THE INTIMATE LIFE OF
SIR WALTER SCOTT

AGENTS

AMERICA . . . THE MACMILLAN COMPANY
64 & 66 FIFTH AVENUE, NEW YORK

AUSTRALASIA . OXFORD UNIVERSITY PRESS
205 FLINDERS LANE, MELBOURNE

CANADA . . . . THE MACMILLAN COMPANY OF CANADA, LTD.
ST. MARTIN'S HOUSE, 70 BOND STREET, TORONTO

INDIA . . . . MACMILLAN & COMPANY, LTD.
MACMILLAN BUILDING, BOMBAY
309 BOW BAZAAR STREET, CALCUTTA

THE INTIMATE LIFE

OF

SIR WALTER SCOTT

BY

ARCHIBALD STALKER

A. & C. BLACK LTD.

4, 5 & 6 SOHO SQUARE, LONDON, W 1.

1921

CONTENTS

CHAP.   PAGE

   I. By Way of Introduction 1

  II. Father and Mother 4

 III. Boyhood and Youth 16

 IV. First Love 26

  V. Lady Scott of Abbotsford 34

 VI. Interesting People associated with Scott . . 42

VII. The Personality of Sir Walter 62

VIII. The Personality of Sir Walter (continued) . . 77

 IX. The Children 84

  X. Family Life at Abbotsford 98

 XI. Tom Purdie, the Friend and Tyrant . . . 121

XII. A Day at Abbotsford 129

XIII. The Ballantynes and the Businesses . . . 144

XIV. The Ballantynes and the Businesses (continued) . 154

 XV. Scott as a Literary Man 163

XVI. His Social and Political Views 174

XVII. The Disaster of 1826 192

    Index 205

NOTE

THE chapter on Sir Walter's Father and Mother has appeared in *The Cornhill Magazine*; that on Tom Purdie has been published in *Chambers's Journal*, and that on Sir Walter's First Love in *The Scots Pictorial*.

I acknowledge, with thanks, the permission of the Proprietors and Editors of the three magazines to republish these chapters.

A. S.

EDINBURGH,
 1st January 1921.

THE INTIMATE LIFE OF
SIR WALTER SCOTT

CHAPTER I

BY WAY OF INTRODUCTION

THERE have been many Lives of Scott, though there is only one *Life*, which is Lockhart's; and considering the number of those Lives and the fact that it is nearly a hundred years since Sir Walter died, the natural inquiry of the twentieth centurion is, " What is there new to say about Scott ? Is there anything new ? "

There is, indeed, a great deal that has never been interpreted before, and there is still more that has never yet received the emphasis it deserves; but there is another consideration. Readers of books are yet alive who remember the time when it was still considered ridiculous to take Sir Walter's own estimate of his literary value. Year by year the world has been coming round to his way of thinking, and those who go to gaze now on the bright landscape he created on Tweed can join with him in his profound estimate of the tasks he did—" My oaks will outlast my laurels."

But just because his long poems are uninspired, and because people after a hundred years have admitted the truth of his opinion that what he called his " big bow-wow " method of writing prose was apt to become intolerable, there is room for a new estimate of Sir Walter. After all, let the literary say what they please, books are a small affair, and this was Sir Walter's opinion as well as mine. Architecture, sculpture, music, have profundities and sublimities that . . . At any rate, life is more than books, and, though Sir Walter's have lost a good deal of their freshness, his joyous personal life, which has never before been told as a consecutive narrative, has lost not a shade of its brightness. That is the justification of this book.

For this presentation of Sir Walter is new. It is not the picture of him that is given in the books of last century, and it may be unsatisfactory in the eyes of 2020, but it is a twentieth-century portrait that contains lights and shadows obscure or absent in previous representations. This is the first time, too, that his first love has been discussed with common sense, and that anyone has taken the trouble to master the details of Scott's involved connection with the business firms and with their failure.

It cannot be emphasised too much or too often that Sir Walter thought a great deal more of his daily life, of his friends, sports, plantings and jokes than of books, his own or anybody's else. Accordingly it is not surprising that his books should not have the stuff of endurance in them, nor, on the other hand, is it wonderful that his daily life has provided his most satisfying story. Lockhart, when he wrote the *Life of Scott*, called himself " the compiler of these pages," and substantially he spoke truly. The book is chiefly composed of Scott's letters and journal, though some of Lockhart's own reminiscences are lifelike and poignant.

There is no other biography in our language to touch it except the surpassing *Diary of Samuel Pepys*. Boswell's *Johnson*, if one omits some too meagre details of our dearest Oliver, has always seemed to me rather verbiage for the bookworm than the substance of life, though a masterpiece of presentation. *The Life of Scott* is Scott's best book. He lived it and he wrote it, a story that I can hardly imagine England or Scotland growing weary of.

I have repeated few of the best-known stories told by or about Scott, but some of these ancient favourites have been essential to the presentation of his intimate life. Much material has been found in footnotes, asides, and stray places that reveal by accident the spirit and substance of the household, while all the mental energy of the writer is concentrated on the elaboration of matters of gravity and unimportance.

Even when Scott kept a daily journal he was reticent about his personal life. He knew Pepys, as far as Pepys was then published, and delighted in his domesticities and open confessions, but in this matter Pepys had no influence on him. There was a curious dignity of bearing about that age. The ceremonious manner of the eighteenth century, which had been allied with such plainness of speech and writing that its commonest words are now the shocking part of our language, continued into the nineteenth century. The plainness of speech was continued in private company, but it became indecorous, for instance, to " intrude on the sanctities of private life." I found by accident, in a casual remark of Hogg's, that Scott at table was accustomed to set the company in a roar over Charles's latest boyish cleverness or blunder, but it is certain that he would have thought it not only rude but wrong if the child's exquisite speeches had been noted in the journal of any of his guests, and he himself never mentioned them in his letters or his journal. This spirit of reticence, which was only a passing characteristic of that generation, is responsible for the loss of thousands of pleasant anecdotes about Scott and his daily life.

CHAPTER II

FATHER AND MOTHER

IT has been said that the fathers and mothers of men of genius are themselves invariably of extraordinary character, but probably if a sympathetic record were made of any father and mother in the world they would be found to have many striking and original points. This is certainly the utmost that can be said of Walter Scott the elder and Anne Rutherford his wife. They present clear but not extraordinary personalities; they were brave and scrupulous and honest, content with appalling Presbyterian routine; they found their pleasures in strange but respectable places, and in spite of plentiful cash and prosperity were on the whole as unhappy as the rest of mankind.

Walter Scott the elder was born in 1729. His father was Farmer Robert of Sandyknowe, a calculating man who realised that a Borderer in the legal profession would do exceedingly well among the wealthy peers and the quarrelsome lairds and farmers of Berwick, Roxburgh and Dumfries. Recall Dandie Dinmont's final excuse for going to law, after several fights with Jock o' Dawston Cleugh, about his boundary, the difference amounting to the feeding of one sheep : " Besides, a man's aye the better thought o' in our country for having been afore the Fifteen," that is, for having a lawsuit in the Court of Session at Edinburgh. So young Walter, the eldest of the family, was duly sent to the capital and apprenticed to an attorney there. His father paid the handsome sum required of solicitors who join the Society of Writers to the Signet—at present it is about £500—bought him also a partnership with another W.S., and the Border connection brought him an extensive practice.

His portrait shows a face of soft sweetness and melancholy,

decidedly a conscientious face. He was noted among all his acquaintance for gentleness. Sir Walter said that his father's face and figure were uncommonly handsome, that his manners were rather formal—to the twentieth century this would mean a lot more than it meant in 1808 when Sir Walter wrote—and that his habits were abstemious, though when on occasion wine was produced a single glass or two exhilarated him greatly.

Mrs. Cockburn, the lady who spoiled the ancient ballad of *The Flowers of the Forest* and did worse by providing occasion for the supersession of the exquisite ancient melody—now raising itself again—was one of his early friends. Among the serious amusements at the parties of that young generation were toasts laboriously prepared beforehand in descriptive verse, and with no names mentioned. It was a point of honour that recognition of the description should be instantaneous and unanimous. Think of the pride of the young lawyer when he heard the following verses of Mrs. Cockburn's recited, and when the company, as generous of mind as himself, rose to their feet and all together pointing to him shouted, " To Walter Scott ! " :

> " To a thing that's uncommon,
>   A youth of discretion,
> Who though vastly handsome
>   Despises flirtation ;
> To the friend in affliction,
>   The heart of affection
> Who may hear the last trump
>   Without dread of detection."

In April 1758, when he was about twenty-nine, he married Anne Rutherford, eldest daughter of Dr. John Rutherford, professor of medicine in Edinburgh University. She was then either eighteen or nineteen. Her mother was a Swinton, and had died early ; her father had married again and had or was even to have several other children, one of whom, Christian Rutherford, the dearly loved Miss Christie, was to be to Sir Walter rather a sister than an aunt.

Even Lockhart significantly says that Anne Rutherford " was short of stature and by no means comely." It would hardly have been natural for the handsome Walter to have mated with his own type, and the world has good reason to thank him : he chose well. Her portrait shows her very plain indeed, with a sagacious face that I am sure could light up with laughter nearly as luminously as her son's. She had a light and happy temper, had great pleasure in verse, and was, as the respectable of her generation in Scotland all were, a bit religious.

She had had what was considered a good education, and was " finished off " by the Hon. Mrs. Ogilvie, a lady who trained her pupils to a style of manners which was very soon to be considered intolerably stiff. It is said that women live greatly on the memory of a good school. This is not true of those women who fall in love joyously and once for ever in youth, but of others it may be very true. It certainly must have been true of Anne Scott. So intensely was this correct-ness of school deportment burned into the souls of those children that even when about eighty years old Mrs. Scott took extreme care to avoid touching her chair with her back.

The young couple began their married life in a house or flat belonging to the lawyer in the College Wynd, apparently on the site of the existing Chambers Street, and here thirteen years afterwards Sir Walter was born. But disaster after disaster overwhelmed the bride and bridegroom. All their first *six* children were born alive and perished in infancy. It is curious that Sir Walter was the second child to be named Walter and that Robert, the eldest who survived, was the third who bore that name. Apparently Walter Scott the elder was not easily frightened by superstitious notions of ill-luck, but he did ultimately come to the conclusion that the confined surroundings and general lack of sanitation of College Wynd were responsible for the deaths of his children. Accordingly in 1771, shortly after Walter was born, the family removed to George Square, a locality which even yet is roomy and open. About that time there was a general exodus of the upper classes from the huge tenements of the walled city, with its manure-heaps on the streets, and with its roaming fat pigs on whose backs might occasionally be seen the future leaders of fashion, exercising at the age of seven or nine their instincts of publicity. Just then began the building of the spacious and stately New

Town of Edinburgh, the plan of which as an example of civics before 1800 is even more worthy of the attention of strangers than the Castle and Holyrood, and is a great contrast to the narrow and confined development of the city since then.

Mrs. Scott's father, the professor of medicine, lectured to his students in Latin. When prescribing for his patients it was his custom at the same time to offer a prayer for the accompanying blessing of heaven, " a laudable practice," says the Rev. Mr. Mitchell, the tutor of the children, " in which I fear he has not been generally imitated by those of his profession." The reverend gentleman afterwards obtained a church in Montrose, and got " an electrical shock " when Walter Scott, advocate, spent a night at Montrose and said that he was collecting " ancient ballads and traditional stories about fairies, witches and ghosts." This was the gentleman who wrote that *he was generally given to understand* that the Novels were of a more pure and unexceptionable nature than characterised other writings of the kind.

But I return to the prayer from which the reverend gentleman, one of a thousand beautiful characters associated with Scott, beguiled us. Professor Rutherford no doubt increased the number of his patients by his addition to the dreary routine of his half-dozen prescriptions. Picture the sensations of the patient of to-day, who in such a manner should have his faith in the infallible bottle destroyed by the prescriber himself.

Of the six children who survived and matured one was a girl, Anne, a year younger than Sir Walter, who observed that from her cradle she was the hunted victim of mischance, that her childhood was full of escapes from the most perilous accidents, maiming, burning, drowning, and that she lived chiefly in a world of her own imagination. She was never well, and she died at twenty-nine.

Robert, the eldest of the family, entered the Navy, but quarrelled with his fellow-officers and resigned. He joined the East India Company's service and died of fever before 1808, when he could not have been more than forty-one.

John, the second, was born about 1769. He got a commission in the Army, but when campaigning ruined his health he retired with the rank of major and stayed in Edinburgh with his mother. He died in 1816 at the age of forty-seven.

Thomas, the poet's favourite brother, was two years younger than he. He inherited the law business of his father, speculated, failed, fled, and after some vicissitudes died in 1823 at the age of fifty.

Lastly, the youngest of the family, Daniel, the black sheep and the heart-break, died before he was thirty, leaving as a last blow to the proud family an illegitimate son whom Mrs. Scott either took into her house or supported elsewhere till she died. At her death Walter, who had refused even to go to Daniel's funeral, a frightful blow from a Scott, became responsible for the boy's support.

It is difficult to give a complete picture of the household at George Square as the children grew up. The intense care and watchfulness of the mother and the anxiety of the father may be assumed from their pathetic search for a cure of the lameness that resulted from Walter's acute poliomyelitis or infantile paralysis. Few things that money could supply, however, were lacking to the children of the prosperous attorney. As the boys grew he gave them a tutor who lived in the house with them. Walter at one time had lessons in painting and drawing from two different masters, though he afterwards said that he could make progress in neither. A singing-master was provided for the children, and as is so often the case with instruction in the arts in this island, it was wasted. The lady next door, exasperated at the yowls of the young Scotts, sent a message begging that the children might not *all* be flogged precisely at the same hour, because the noise when they yelled together was really dreadful, though, she added, no doubt their punishment was deserved. Robert was the only one of the six who could sing.

Walter Scott, senior, was intensely religious. He and his wife were Presbyterian of the Presbyterians and took their family to the long sermons of the kirk at least twice every Sunday. On the Sunday evenings father and mother sat in their chairs in the drawing-room of a darkened silent house, surrounded by the whole roll of the children. The father read a long gloomy sermon from beginning to inexorable end.

Then . . . another. And another. The servants were called in, and both servants and children were examined on the Church catechism and on the two sermons they had heard at church. The children and servants disposed of, the family tutor, who had passed through the theological college but had not yet succeeded in obtaining a church, examined the head of the house and the lady, and " concluded with prayer."

Walter, the boy with the marvellous memory, rather puzzled his father at these Sunday evening examinations. He was always of a drowsy disposition, and in spite of example and precept he slept in church. Apparently he listened to the text and to the preacher's preliminary statement of the divisions he proposed to discuss, then settled to sleep : his imagination or experience or possibly a few odd moments of wakefulness supplied the rest, for he was always ready to tell everything the minister had said—an example to the other children of the intellectual benefits of sleep.

In early manhood, when writing to Miss Christie, he let himself go on the subject of the Fast week which preceded the half-yearly communion. " This being sermon week we are looking very religious and very sour at home. However, it is with some folk that in proportion as they are pure themselves they are entitled to render uncomfortable those whom they consider less perfect." This is a hit at his father.

These were Sir Walter's boyhood Sundays. The impatient, silent children endured them with rebellion in their hearts, and awaited the moment when the intolerable gloom would lift and they would be allowed to breathe the clear air of *The Pilgrim's Progress* and one half-dozen other permitted books, or at least would be allowed to talk. Looking back on it all from his serene manhood and from his success, Sir Walter dismissed the sombre repression with impatient contempt. " In the end it did none of us any good," he said.

It was partly an affair of the age and partly an expression of the temperament of the Writer to the Signet. He was a very serious man. Curious to think of a W.S. sitting alone in his *real* study, where he must not be disturbed (no golf links, theatres, week-ends or even dinners in his mind), and supposed by wife and children to be busy over Dirleton's *Doubts* or

Stair's *Decisions*, heavy lawbooks, but really wrapt up in complete enjoyment hour after hour of Spottiswood's or Woodrow's theological works.

A rich farmer about Haddington who had a case in the Court of Session came up from the country and approached Walter Scott, senior, one Sunday, asking for a look at the papers in the case. The Sabbatarian lawyer suggested that the next day would do equally well, but the client was not to be denied. Scott found the papers, delivered them to the farmer, and said that it was not his habit to do business on Sundays, but added a trifle bitterly that the farmer would have no difficulty in finding lawyers in Edinburgh who would have no such scruple ; and so he washed his hands of a good case.

His religion must have meant a great deal to him, but in one instance it appeared to affect his judgment. Scott himself told Lockhart that it was a common thing at table, if anybody said that the soup was good, for his father to taste it again and say, " Yes, it is too good, bairns ! " and pour a tumbler of cold water into his own plate.

Apparently if attention had not been called to the merits of the soup, Scott would have enjoyed it warm and flavoured, but simply because attention was drawn to its goodness he sacrificed it to the envious gods.

He was not an absolute bigot : though religious he apparently gave way to reason in play-acting, the special horror and ignorance of the pious of that age. The children had their own little theatricals in the dining-room, and were countenanced if not encouraged. When they tackled scenes from Richard III. it was Walter who remarked that he would do Gloucester, because the limp would do well enough to represent the hump.

In those days a successful lawyer thought it a shame that a beggar (though duly licensed to beg) should have mutton to his dinner, whether his begging was successful or not. Let those who do not know or do not remember the exquisite story of Scott and the old Bluegown beggar read it in chapter vi. of Lockhart's *Life*. The point I wish to make is its more exquisite conclusion. Walter told his mother how he had dined off a gigot of mutton, potatoes and whisky (he was nineteen) at the house of his fellow-student, son of the beggar, and asked her whether the student could be preferred to a place as tutor in some gentleman's family. He suggested that his father would have influence enough, but his mother's knowledge of his father made an unexpected objection.

" Dinna speak to your father about it," she said. " If it had been a shoulder he might have thought less, *but he will say the gigot was a sin*. I'll see what I can do." And sure enough her minister got the lad a position as tutor.

But Mrs. Scott was able to take extreme liberties with her husband when she cared. A sedan chair came to the house door every evening of one autumn and a man, very much muffled, came out of it, was immediately ushered into the lawyer's study, and worked there with him till long after the bedtime of the rest of the family. Mrs. Scott repeatedly asked who and what he was, but the lawyer evaded her inquiries and told her nothing. Another man would have gone to his office and would have received his visitor there, but the open-hearted lawyer was not built that way. He told his wife that the man was not worth bothering about, and refused to discuss him. To this generation, when it is believed that Cabinet ministers inform not only their wives but even their newspapers of anything and everything of importance, this distaste or distrust seems strange, and still more curious appears the independent way in which Mrs. Scott solved the problem.

One evening just as the stranger was about to go she went into the room and made a little speech about the cup of tea she brought on a tray. So she got a good stare at the stranger. Thunder sat on her meek husband's brow and he refused to take the tea, but the well-mannered stranger took his. He was Murray of Broughton, who had been secretary to Prince Charles, and whose evidence had sent many to the scaffold. Walter Scott though apparently bound to do some business with him, detested him, and would not show him any hospitality nor exchange any act of friendship with him.

When he left the lawyer opened the window and flung into the street the cup from which the stranger had drunk.

How limited the amusements of this conscientious lawyer

were, and how painstaking his son was, another anecdote shows. Walter copied out twice his notes of the Scots Law class, had one set of volumes bound, and gave them to his father. The old man declared that he was highly pleased with them, not only as proof of Walter's assiduity but because the lectures would give him very pleasant reading for leisure hours.

He positively loved funerals. The man who had buried his six firstborn might have had enough of the ceremonies attendant on death, but his appetite for melancholy grew with indulgence. This is common in Scotland, and probably elsewhere. One aspect of the attraction of funerals is illustrated in the story of the working farmer, who cautiously approached his one ploughman with news of a soirée.

"And whit aboot Jock's funeral?" asked the canny ploughman.

"I thocht o' gaein to Jock's funeral mysel'," ventured the farmer.

"I winna hae't. There's mair fun at ae guid funeral than at fifty sorrees."

It was not the whisky and the dinner, however, but the sombre pageant that appealed to the lawyer. He cut a stately figure in his black kneebreeches, with laced coat and ruffles, and he enjoyed himself immensely. He kept a long list of cousins, second-cousins, cousins by marriage and other remote relations continually in countenance, and his son's opinion was that this interest in them was chiefly to attend their funerals, *some of which he even paid for*. Considering what funerals were in the eighteenth century, this must have been an expensive hobby.

It is difficult at times to regard the ways of Providence with patience. Who does not know men of sixty and seventy, even one or two of eighty, who are with impunity gluttonous, hard drinkers, self-indulgent? Yet it was to this conscientious, abstemious man of regular habits that apoplexy, popularly supposed to be the result of over-indulgence, came at the age of sixty-eight. For two years he lingered, irritable with everybody, thankless, passionate, driving the household distracted, while the undaunted little wife and mother, daughterless though she was, attended on him and sacrificed herself to him.

There is not much said by Lockhart about the relations of father and son, but I suspect that there was some estrangement, and that there were occasional rows even before the father's shock. The father objected to the son's walking tours, especially when he went off for a day and stayed for a week, objected also to Walter's lack of concentration. He appears to have objected heartily and openly to the publication of verse by the young advocate, and I have little doubt that the poet's lack of success at the Bar worried the ageing father greatly. On the other side the son objected to the sourness and gloom of the religious observances forced by the elder on the whole household, and when he lost both parents it was chiefly his mother's memory that he cherished. His letter to her, written from London when he got the news of his father's death, is an appalling document :

" Your own principles of virtue and religion will, I well know, be your best support in this heaviest of human afflictions. The removal of my regretted parent from this earthly scene is to him doubtless the happiest change. . . ."

There is a terrible paragraph of sixteen words in Lockhart. After illustrating the burden that old Walter during his illness was to his family, treating his womenfolk to passionate outbursts and continual unreasonableness, he adds :

" I have lived to see the curtain rise and fall once more on a like scene."

Anne Scott lived for twenty years and a half after her husband. The house that for two years had been all gloom brightened again ; she received visitors, especially delighted in Walter's children, and opened her maternal heart to nurse another strong man fallen by the wayside, her son John, who retired from the Army broken in health. He, too, died before her, and at the age of seventy-nine or eighty she was his constant nurse.

She had about £300 a year, of which a good third went in charities of her own. On the remainder she was able to keep a quietly hospitable house. Out of his superabundance Sir

Walter often offered her assistance, which she scornfully and affectionately refused every time. She lived to see her lame son a baronet, to read not only his verses but his novels, and to point out to her visitors the discrepancies between Walter's plots and the real stories. He attributed a good deal of his knowledge of the manners and habits of the two or three preceding generations to her conversation. She had a fine memory and a gift for telling stories, had all the Scottish passion for genealogy, and could rattle off the ancestry of everybody she knew or had ever heard of. She had proverbs also for every occasion, and two of them were often in Sir Walter's mouth :

" We must do as we *dow*," that is, as we can do, and

> " Well betides
> Her that bides."

Both of these illustrate a patient mind and a happy knack of minimising present trouble.

On a Saturday in December 1819 the baronet visited his mother and found her well. Next day the girls Sophia and Anne had tea with her, and found the old lady in fine spirits, telling her best stories over again with great gusto, as we all do. On the Monday she had a seizure. Helpless, but apparently suffering no pain, she gradually slept away on Christmas Eve.

A few days before her death the trembling hand of eighty had inscribed her dearest possession, a large Bible in two volumes and a gift from her father, " To my dear son, Walter Scott, from his affectionate mother, Anne Rutherford."

It gave Sir Walter an exquisite pang of grief when he came into her house after she had for ever parted from him, to behold the array of presents that she had bought or made ready with her hands for him and the rest of her dear ones against the New Year. His letter to Lady Louisa Stuart telling her of his mother's death is tender and proud and homely, a beautiful expression of affection.

When in September 1832, merely thirteen years afterwards, Sir Walter's own executors, searching for his will, opened his desk, they found arranged in it in careful order a series of articles that had apparently been placed so that he might have them before his eyes as he began his morning tasks. These were the old-fashioned boxes that had stood on his mother's dressing-table which he had studied a thousand times when as a sickly child he had slept in her bedroom ; the silver taper-stand that he had bought her with his first five-guinea fee ; his father's snuff-box and etui-case and other such things.

This is, on the whole, a sombre record, but that is because the recorded facts are chiefly sombre. I have little doubt that Walter and Anne Scott enjoyed their lives. In his prime the lawyer was continually touring the Borders on business —and then he had his funerals ; in her maturity the mother of the famous Walter must have had intense pride in his fame and success, though this was utterly denied to her husband. Much more she had to rejoice in, with much to sorrow over. Anyway at the age of eighty she was happy pouring out tea for her grandchildren, telling them her favourite stories and enjoying the bright courtesy of their youthfulness. I am convinced that to herself her life was a satisfactory one.

CHAPTER III

BOYHOOD AND YOUTH

WALTER was a healthy baby, and, like many other infants, he ran some risks and sustained much damage before he got even as far as trousers. His first wet-nurse had consumption, but her doctor was a friend of old Walter's and put him on his guard. At eighteen months the child took infantile paralysis, and on the fourth day of the fever it was discovered when he was being bathed that he had lost the power of his right leg. The anxious parents not only then but for many years afterwards tried every cure they heard of, but the nearest they came to a cure was grandfather Dr. Rutherford's advice to send him into the country. So Walter went to stay at grandfather Robert's farmhouse at Sandyknowe.

At Sandyknowe he had his first consciousness and his first recollections. His grandmother told him many a story of the Border thieves, and Aunt Janet Scott read the few farmhouse books for him with a patience which responded to every appeal, and which the fathers and mothers of bright boys may well admire from a distance.

When he was three the waters of Bath were recommended for the shrunken limb, and Aunt Janet, the lady of the out-of-the-world farmhouse, went with him to crowded fashionable Bath to try them. But he got no good from the waters nor from a year's stay there; the leg remained shrunken, though the child's health continued to improve. Bath, however, was memorable because of the arrival of Uncle Robert, who loved Walter all his life, and who, as early as this, set himself to amuse the child. With Uncle Robert he went for the first time in his life to the theatre, and at the age of four enjoyed *As You Like It*.

At six he got his first pony, a tiny Shetland mare, the

gift of Uncle Thomas Scott. The little mare walked freely
into the house at Sandyknowe, and Walter regularly fed her
there from his own hand. Fifty years afterwards he was to
give his grandson a little Shetland mare, and was to call her
Marion in remembrance of the favourite of his own boyhood.

He himself recognised a lifelong characteristic in a story
that he used to tell of his sixth year. Two servant girls at
Sandyknowe, after putting him to bed, sat down by his nursery
fire. In the course of their talk one began to tell a most
dismal ghost story, of which Walter remembered the beginning
all his life. Being afraid, however, of what was to come, he
ducked his head beneath the blankets and escaped it.

At seven or eight he was discussing the American War with
an old ensign who possessed maps, was prophesying trouble
for Burgoyne, and was looked upon by the ancient as an
uncanny imp of darkness when Burgoyne came to trouble
indeed. At this age, too, he was transferred for good back
to his father's house in Edinburgh, and felt severely the
change from being the only and the spoiled child of a household to becoming one among half a dozen riotous and self-
willed Scotts. He was sent to the High School, and the tutor
at home helped with his lessons; but when Walter took down
the fascinating old *Chronicles of Lindsay of Pitscottie*, the
reverend tutor gently put it back and made him learn by
heart " Rollin's infernal list of the Shepherd Kings, whose
hard names could have done no good to any one on earth."

The tutor, however, could not restrain this lad's native
tastes. Even as a small boy he was familiar with George
Constable, an antiquary, and with Dr. Blacklock, a forgotten
minor poet, both of whom put him on the track of books in
prose and verse, and lent him their volumes freely.

In those days, and for long afterwards, boys of eleven
and twelve went to the university and began to learn the
Greek alphabet. Scott went when he was about thirteen,
and about the same time he began to develop his general
health. Indeed, the lame boy became a very fit walker, and
with his constant companion, John Irving, often walked out
to Roslin, down the Esk to Lasswade, and home before dinner,
a tramp of a good dozen miles. A factory now shuts off part

2

of the river from the public, but those who have observed the beautiful details of the little church, or from a distance have caught its proportion, no less beautiful ; those, too, who have walked down Roslin dell in the months of the spring wild flowers, or in June when a thousand tints of green on the Hawthornden woods across the river shine in the sun, can understand why Walter " was specially fond of Roslin."

The whole course of his education was fragmentary. He attended the High School of Edinburgh ; for the first year or two he went to a private school for an hour or two a day, and he shared the attentions of the private tutor at home ; but he was careless and idle, as a boy of his brooding temperament was bound to be. At the university he took the classes necessary to prepare him for his advocate's examination, but he did not take a degree.

At fifteen he entered into indentures with his father, and the desk of the law-apprentice, who could drudge with the best when he made up his mind, was always full of books— not of law-books. In the days of his apprenticeship his chief friend and companion remained John Irving of the walks, who afterwards became a solicitor and Writer to the Signet, and of whom he did not see a great deal after he became an advocate. With John he read a great deal, and learnt enough Italian to go through Ariosto and other romantics.

Tom was the favourite of his father, but Walter was the particular favourite of his mother. Her salutation of him even when he was a six-foot man, a baronet, a father, and famous all over the world, was invariably, " Wattie, my lamb." The lameness of the child had made an indelible impression of pity on her heart, and when her eldest son Robert, went off to the Navy and John went to the Army she openly rejoiced that Walter was lame and would not be accepted for either. There is no doubt that if he had been eligible he would have gone to the Army, for his heart was there all his days.

When Robert first gave signs of desire for the Navy, Mrs Scott was distraught. She persuaded an old sailor to come and tell, by way of warning, his wildest stories of wreck and drowning. The good children gathered round with ecstasy and the more horrors he related the better they were pleased. He did not keep Robert from the Navy for an hour, and he gave little Walter merely more regrets.

At sixteen the boy broke a blood-vessel in his bowels, and lay in bed during a cold spring, with only one blanket, was bled and blistered, was fed only on vegetables, and was not allowed to talk. He was permitted, however, to read and to play chess; he devoured scores of books, and made a slow recovery. And all the while his parents hoped against hope that something or other would turn up to cure his lameness. They tried electrical treatment; they tried earth-baths, and the recipes, outward and inward, of every quack who shouted promises for a living.

After the spring illness he went for convalescence to Rosebank, near Kelso, a fine house just taken by Uncle Robert Scott. Here he returned again and again when home grew too much to endure, and speedily became Uncle Robert's boy. Here he began shooting, and was one of those who have exterminated the heron, which was common round about Kelso in his time. From his uncle he acquired the taste for exploring battle-grounds, old forts and antiquities; from him, too, he received encouragement to read and to versify. The relatives who influenced him and developed his special characteristics were indeed not few, but he received no assistance from his father; their tastes and pursuits were actually antagonistic. And his father worried himself by taking the eternal and wrong-headed view of parents, that if a child does not pursue success by the means approved by the parent, but in its own way, it does wrong.

His mother influenced him greatly; so did Aunt Janet and Grandmother Scott at Sandyknowe. Christie Rutherford, the aunt who was just a year or two older than himself, deserves mention with George Constable. He had crowds of aunts, cousins and second-cousins, of whom, as a boy, he saw a good deal. Among these relatives may be mentioned Grand-aunt Swinton, who lived near George Square, and who was always pulled out of her own house into the George Square nursery when any of the children were ill. When they were tired of play they ran into her house calling for a story; and she was ready for them, for she was an old lady of some reading and character.

Other forces went to the moulding of his mind. It was not uncommon for the boys of fifteen and sixteen to be asked to dinner-parties and receptions where there were boys of their own age in the family. They were expected to be silent, but they were allowed their fair share of claret or even of port. In this way Scott at sixteen or so saw many of the celebrities of his day, and listened to a great deal of conversation on subjects dear to him at an age when other boys are groping for guidance in the dark.

A word from Charles Kirkpatrick Sharpe about the girls of Scott's time is worth quoting as demonstrating the free and easy upbringing of the aristocracy of Scotland in that generation. " I myself remember some now very fine Scotch ladies who used to scud about without stockings when they were past fifteen."

At seventeen, Scott went to the Civil Law classes and began to associate with some of the advocates of the future, George Cranstoun, George Abercromby, J. J. Edmonstone, two Murrays, Will Clerk and others. With them he went not to one but to several debating societies, and with them he got drunk regularly. " That he partook profusely in the juvenile bacchanalia of that day, and continued to take a plentiful share in such jollities down to the time of his marriage, are facts worthy of being distinctly stated," says Lockhart plainly, and Scott often said and wrote the same thing. It was a custom of the time, though an expiring one, and in middle age there were few men of strong constitution so temperate (in everything but breakfast) as Scott.

When the time came to warn his own eldest boy against the dangers of life, he wrote : " I am sorry and ashamed to say for your warning that the habit of drinking wine, so much practised when I was a young man, occasioned, I am convinced, many of my cruel stomach complaints." With all this drinking there was naturally a good deal of quarrelling, and Walter's gentle firmness in settling disputes was often in request.

Nineteen of those boys set up a Club of their own, and met on Friday evenings in a room in Carrubber's Close. After discussion they, or at any rate those of them who had pocket-money, usually went for supper to an oyster tavern near by. Year after year the members who were in Edinburgh dined together at the close of the winter and summer sessions of the law courts, and during thirty years Sir Walter was very seldom absent. It was a rule, too, that when any member received an appointment or promotion he should give a dinner to the rest, and Sir Walter gave two such dinners, one when he became Sheriff, and the other when he became Clerk of Session.

At nineteen he joined the Speculative Society, the play-ground of advocates in training, and here he met Jeffrey, afterwards his friend in society and his antagonist in literature and politics.

Jeffrey looked him up shortly after becoming acquainted with him and found him in his study, in the basement of the George Square house. The basement den was base indeed, but was all his own. A cabinet of Scotch and Roman coins, a claymore and Lochaber axe, gifts of old Stewart of Inver-nahyle, a print of Prince Charlie, and a host of books without shelves, made in their way a queer and pathetic nest of eggs out of which were hatched the magnificent library, the hall and the museum of Abbotsford.

The society of Edinburgh at that time retained much of Scottish simplicity. Sedan-chairs were just out of fashion and carriages were little used, for the narrow streets would hardly allow two to pass, and the houses of earls and law lords were oftener than not approached through " pends," closes or entrances through which a carriage simply could not go. Accordingly, till the migration to the new town was nearly complete, ladies and their escorts used to walk to dinner-parties and balls, with lanterns or torches to light the way when necessary; and it was an evening entertainment for the public to watch parties of well-dressed women and men going by.

Walter had a good time out of town as well as in town. His description of the simple life on the Borders is enough to make famished city-dwellers envy its luxuriousness. He was on the English side of the Cheviots with Uncle Robert, who paid the expenses, in August 1791 when he was just twenty, and was enjoying himself fishing, shooting and exploring the old battle-grounds.

" My uncle drinks the whey here, as I do ever since I understood it was brought to his bedside every morning at six by a very pretty dairymaid. We dine and sup upon fish from the stream, and the most delicious heath-fed mutton, barn-door fowls, pies, milk-cheese, etc., all in perfection ; and so much simplicity resides among these hills that a pen, one which could write at least, was not to be found about the house, though belonging to a considerable farmer, till I shot the crow with whose quill I write this epistle."

He was admitted an advocate before he was quite twenty one, but had only two days at Court before the summer recess. A friendly solicitor gave him a guinea fee on his first day, but nothing of importance detained him, and after his hard study he was glad to get away to Rosebank for a long holiday. Uncle Robert took him for the second or third time into Northumberland to explore the country there. He stayed at least six weeks with Uncle Robert, and early in October he was introduced at Jedburgh to Robert Shortreed, then or later Sheriff substitute of Roxburghshire. Scott found that Shortreed had many friends and relatives in wild Liddesdale, and knew the long dale on the borders well by personal exploration. Their plans fitted, and off they went together, Shortreed glad of a holiday and young Scott especially enthusiastic over the ballads he was sure to pick up from the remote Borderers.

The Border visit was a great success. They were made welcome among Shortreed's friends, relatives and clients everywhere. Sometimes they slept in a cottar's house : frequently they dined at some manse or other, and often had carousal in a farmer's house at night. Their total expenses on this first journey were for two feeds of corn that the horse had at Riccarton Mill going and coming. It was an age of tolls, and even thirty years later Mrs. Hughes, going across a bridge from her inn to get her carriage-horses changed, paid 5s. 4d. for doing so ; but Scott and Shortreed paid not one penny in tolls—that is to say, they never rode on a road at the time, for there were no roads.

In a later year when Scott went on a similar wild journey with Leyden they ate braxy—dead sheep—and occasionally slept on top of peat-stacks, for there were no inns. But for seven successive years Shortreed and he went happily on Liddesdale holidays, and not only had fine times, but obtained much of the material that was to be *The Minstrelsy of the Scottish Border*.

When he returned to Parliament House he was not long of establishing a reputation, among the bewigged and gowned advocates who tramp the floor there, as a fine teller of stories, but he made little progress in law. No cases came his way, and he found more pleasure in a German class which was attended by most of his friends. This was the first time that German was ever taught in Scotland.

In the following spring a law case was entrusted to him; the case of a drunken minister who was dismissed. In May the trial was heard, and Walter's friends, the other young advocates, came in a troop to the gallery of the small court-room. He began in a low voice, but gained confidence as he went on, and at length when he had to repeat some of the minister's alleged indecent speeches he enunciated them so heartily that an old judge on the bench called him to order with rebuke in his voice. At this Walter grew confused, and when by and by he had to quote one of the minister's drinking-songs he hesitated over it and lowered his voice. Hereupon the youths in the gallery, deeming that he needed encouragement, scandalised the Court by shouting, " Hear, hear ! " " Encore, encore ! " They were immediately turned out, and Scott finished his speech " very little to his own satisfaction." The minister was deposed.

He believed that he had been a complete failure, and it took all the sympathy of his friends to cheer him up.

In the summer in which he was twenty-two he went round Perthshire and Stirlingshire with his fast friend, Adam Fergusson, staying chiefly at the houses of advocate friends, and making excursions that he was afterwards to make good use of in his verses. The following winter he was again at the German class and at the Speculative Society debates, and was also developing great interest in criminal trials. The brutality of the most brutal criminals always had a kind of fascination for him.

On one occasion he took food with him or got it brought to him, and sat in court for nineteen hours on end, from seven o'clock one morning till two the next, to watch the trial of some political wretches, including a Government spy who had been underpaid and had played his employers false. He was not interested in the law of the case, but in the crimes and the politics. He complained in later years when he had to attend regularly for four hours a day or less, of the stifling fumes of Parliament House, so nineteen hours of it with a crowd packed close must have been a test of endurance even at twenty-three.

At that age he had again an excursion into Perthshire and another to Kelso, going on with Shortreed to Liddesdale as usual. But his other avocations flourished too. He began to make rhymed translations from German, and astonished his friends with them. It may astonish women and men of the age of twenty-three in this generation that when he had translated the *Fiesco* of Schiller the young people to whom he read it sobbed and wept : the reason of their emotion, however, was not in the translation, but in the fact that they all drank too much wine continually, and were always in weeping vein.

Up and down the kingdom volunteering for military duty was the rage, and for a while Scott stood on the pavement enviously watching the infantry, among whom his limp forbade him to march. The formation of troops of light horse in London gave him a cue ; he convened a meeting and suggested the formation of a body of volunteer cavalry. The cavalry was formed, and Scott became quartermaster and secretary ; he was then twenty-five.

The hour of drill was five o'clock in the morning, and though at that time and for a few years afterwards Walter was accustomed to sit up late, he found it no trouble to rise in time for such an early drill. Indeed, he was probably the most enthusiastic of all. Lord Cockburn, in the *Memorials of his Time*, spices a description of Scott's enthusiasm with a trifle of ridicule.

" Walter Scott's zeal in the cause was very curious. He

was the soul of the Edinburgh troop of Midlothian Yeomanry Cavalry. It was not a duty with him, or a necessity, or a pastime, but an absolute passion, indulgence in which gratified his feudal taste for war and his jovial sociableness. He drilled and drank and made songs with a hearty conscientious earnestness which inspired or shamed everybody within the attraction. I do not know if it is usual, but his troop used to practise individually with the sabre at a turnip, which was stuck on the top of a staff to represent a Frenchman in front of the line. Every other trooper when he set forward in his turn was far less concerned about the success of his aim at the turnip, than about how he was to tumble. But Walter frisked forward gallantly, saying to himself, ' Cut them down, the villains ! cut them down ! ' and made his blow, which from his lameness was often an awkward one, cordially, muttering curses all the while at the detested enemy."

The ridicule, however, is quite undeserved. Nobody in his generation had a keener sense of a joke than Walter Scott. The exaggerated earnestness, the dramatic shouts, were the joy of the troop, officers and men. When Knight Walter was on the carpet everybody looked towards him for fun, and this was one of his responses. Finally, when he smote the turnip and rolled off his horse with the vehemence of his blow the laughter and cheers were incense in his nostrils, for he conceived it part of his duty to sustain enthusiasm and joyousness in the troop.

CHAPTER IV

FIRST LOVE

IF the most popular author of to-day had fallen in love, had
been in love for seven years and had been rejected; if scores
of literary men and women of his acquaintance had known all
about it; if he were to die at sixty-one in the fulness of fame,
but leaving many of his confidants behind him, is it possible
that the story of his first love should utterly fail to be recorded
by any person who knew about it or had been told by those
who knew? No! it is impossible, but that is what happened
in the case of Walter Scott and his sweetheart It is possible,
of course, that letters exist which would throw clear light on
the episode, but if they exist they have not been published.
And I must say that I think the jealous delicacy of Scott's
friends a blunder. It is clear from various entries in his
journal that he expected the whole story to be told, and was
proud to think that some day the world would know of his
high and passionate affection.

When he fell in love at nineteen he was an obscure apprentice
of the well-to-do solicitor, his father. He was six feet high,
but not very good-looking, and he limped; but his bright face,
his merry laugh, and his everlasting store of innocent funny
stories made him just the kind of man that ladies love, and
he was not long of discovering that the girl he was so fond
of would rather sit out for an hour on end with him than dance
with anybody else—except, perhaps, one person. Hitherto
he had been rather slovenly in his clothes, but he changed
all that. He had not then the mature neck and jaw that
gave him a Roman head in middle age, but his steady blue
eye, his fine teeth in an age that knew not the dentist, and
his beautifully shaped hands were strong assets, and his
irresistible smile was a provocation to good humour.

It is clear from his youthful letters that the name Greenmantle in *Redgauntlet* was first given to this young lady, and it is recorded that he first spoke to her in Greyfriars Churchyard. No doubt his heart had quickened at sight of her before that rainy Sunday, but it is authentic that he offered her a share of his umbrella as they came out of church, and that their acquaintance began with her acceptance. Sunday after Sunday thereafter they walked back from church together, for their homes were not far apart. The acquaintance of the children led to the meeting of the mothers, who discovered that they had been acquainted as girls. The girl's mother, however, was Lady Jane Stuart, daughter of an earl, and it is probable that her path had been very distant from Anne Rutherford's

The girl was Williamina Belches, daughter of Sir John Belches of Fettercairn, and her prospects of inheritance and marriage were much better than anything young Walter appeared likely to offer. Nobody saw this more clearly than Williamina, but unless she was a born tantaliser it is plain that she only surrendered him with reluctance. In all their companionship, however, she took care not to commit herself definitely, and though Scott, after seven years, could rhyme about his false love, she never accepted an engagement ring from him.

Her portrait shows her a very calculating lady indeed. Pretty there is no doubt she was ; her features were all firm and defined ; her eyes beautifully blue and big ; her face was shapely and decided, no soft sentiment about it. Her hair was dark brown, and in youth she wore it in rings, low at each side of the forehead, parted in the middle, and on festive evenings glistening with jewels. She had a soft flush on her face that deepened when she walked or sang or became animated in any way.

After some time Scott began to meet her in society, and his affection for her was soon a common topic among his acquaintances, girls and men. He wrote verses about her and handed them to Erskine, Clerk, Cranstoun, and to Jane Ann Cranstoun, who was a marvellous girl. He was studying for his advocate's examination, but often when he was supposed to be busiest at his book, he was looking out of the window for a certain blue feather. When the blue feather appeared did he appear too ? I doubt it. He was exceedingly humble with Miss Belches, and humility was, of course, anything but his cue. However, whether continually seeing Walter dashing out of the house after Miss Belches, or in some other way, old Walter slowly realised that here was an acquaintance between boy and girl that might possibly lead to complications. His way of easing his mind on the matter was characteristic of him. He had heard Walter say that he was going on tour in the north, and he realised that the lad would by hook or by crook either get himself invited to Invermay, the country home of the Belches, or would contrive to see a good deal of Williamina at the houses of friends. The Writer to the Signet knew that his son was hardly in a position to aspire to the hand of the baronet's daughter, and he called on the father, explained what he thought was going on, and said that he did not wish the affair to proceed without the sanction of those most interested in the happiness of the children, who were yet too young to calculate consequences for themselves. Though the baronet was astonished, he treated the matter lightly, and thanked the lawyer for his scrupulous attention, but thought there was nothing in the friendship of the boy and girl.

There is little doubt that Williamina heard of this episode from her father. I have as little doubt that her explanation satisfied him. The matter made no difference to Walter, who did not hear of it until long afterwards, and so was spared the anguish of sensitive youth in being made ridiculous by the indelicate delicacy of age.

His aspiration towards the lady did him good in one particular. It was certain that if he remained a solicitor he could stand no chance of marrying her, but as an advocate, in English a barrister, his chance would be much better, so he studied hard and passed his advocate's examinations at the first trial.

His friends, however, thought that he had no chance, and some of them openly told him so, while they did their best to further his cause. His sincere friend, Jane Cranstoun, whose letters are passionate in their clarity and strength, printed at her own expense his earliest mature poem, a translation of Bürger's *Lenore*, for the express purpose of sending a beautifully bound copy to Miss Belches, while Walter and she were staying at the same house in the country.

Mrs. Scott of Harden, a fashionable lady and wife of the Scott whom Walter considered head of his family, took him in hand when he was about twenty-four, gave him a course of deportment and generally polished him up. She told Lockhart, forty years afterwards, that Walter at that time was a bashful and awkward young man; and nothing illustrates this fact so clearly as the uncourageous way in which he made love.

Miss Belches came to Edinburgh only for the winter, and sometimes only for part of it. Accordingly Walter, as the one who was in love, had the opportunities that absence gives to fall in love more deeply, especially as it is unlikely that his chances of seeing her during winter were frequent. But it was natural that the young people should write to each other, and write they did—on literary topics. Miss Belches saw to that; no sentimental correspondence leading up to rash intimate subjects was allowed. So Walter dawdled on till he was twenty-four, and then, instead of putting his arm round her waist, kissing her, and waiting (one instant) to see how she took *that*, as any sensible lover of five years' standing would have done, whether the girl was of his own station or not, instead of that he took the advice of a friend, probably Will Erskine, or David Erskine of Cardross, wrote her a declaration of his undying affection, his urgent desire to marry her, and waited for a reply. And the reply was in the same vein of non-committal willingness as she had shown him all along. What could she have done? The gossip of their small circle infallibly showed her that Walter Scott was making little progress as an advocate, that he had no future to offer a wife, and that to marry him would be the worst of unwisdom. Still, the fortunes of advocates, like those of other men, are sometimes suddenly made. But Walter would have been much better advised to have tried the instinct of a true lover. That instinct is not, " Will the lady listen to my arguments ? " but " Will she be delighted or annoyed if I kiss her ? "

When he received the lady's reply to his declaration he wrote enclosing it to the friend whose feeble advice he followed, telling him that he admired Greenmantle's candour—and would Erskine please say whether the interpretation he took out of it was the same as Walter took ? It gave him the highest satisfaction to find that his friend took the same interpretation out of the reply as he did, and that it was highly flattering and favourable. So it is quite clear that Greenmantle's reply to the poor declaration was not a bit candid, but exceedingly calculated. When he first read it and interpreted it as acceptance, his overwrought spirit, tormented by his determination to harbour no positive hope, found relief in a hearty fit of crying. He was twenty-four and his nights were convivial.

It is only a surmise on my part, but I am convinced of it, for a dozen circumstances point to it. Though Walter had not courage enough to kiss her there was one who had, but then he was a baronet's son, a banker's son, a laird's son, a conquering hero, one William Forbes, whose chief title to remembrance to-day is that he was Scott's good friend, and that he did Scott some kindly services in days of trouble.

The reply to the declaration and offer of marriage apparently was that it would be better to wait a while, to let things go on as they were, not to think of a formal engagement, and (on Walter's part) not to act as though there were one.

This climax of the matter is dated August 1795, when both Walter and Greenmantle were twenty-four. She was sweet to him for another full year, and in the autumn of 1796 he took a holiday in the north and called or stayed at Invermay. The facts were now too plain to be played with, and possibly young Forbes was also in the house. Scott had to be told, and she did not shrink from telling him that she was soon to be married. No explanation of her's has reached us, though we know from Scott's verses that she shed a few tears when she told him she was engaged. He had a servant boy with him, and both were mounted. He rode southwards, put up at Montrose and Perth, and so took his crushed spirit home.

His friends, who had openly prophesied that he was building
on the sands, now dreaded the effect of the rebuff on his constitution, but he had more than the average resilience of youth.
It was in the following spring that he was wild with delight in
volunteering. He was the joy of the parade ground and the
mess ; his laughter and his jokes made him first favourite
with everybody, even with Lieutenant William Forbes,
husband of Williamina, with whom he drilled and dined
daily.

Forbes and she were married in January 1797, but the
lady was not destined to live long. Her husband inherited
the bank, the estate, and the baronetcy of his father, and she
became for a brief while Lady Forbes. Perhaps as she witnessed the meteoric rise of the young poet, his growing importance, his fame, his fortune, she may have experienced
regret, for after all she liked him sincerely.

Scott on his side was convinced that he had been accepted
and jilted, but we realise that he had never been accepted
at all. After he recovered himself he wrote the following
verses :—

> " The violet in her greenwood bower
>   Where birchen boughs with hazels mingle,
> May boast itself the fairest flower
>   In glen or copse or forest-dingle.
>
> Though fair her gems of azure hue
>   Beneath the dewdrop's weight reclining
> I've seen an eye of lovelier blue
>   More sweet through watery lustre shining.
>
> The summer sun that dew shall dry
>   Ere yet the day be past its morrow,
> Nor longer in my false love's eye
>   Remained the tear of parting sorrow."

Greenmantle was married in January and Walter Scott was
married in December of the same year. The society of the
Light Horse in which Scott and Forbes were officers was the
chief resource of both young couples, and they all met once
a week at dinner-parties given by the officers in rotation, but
after a while Mrs. Forbes lived chiefly in the country. It is
almost certain that, though Scott continued to meet Forbes,

and though their families may have met occasionally in company, there was no direct entertainment between them thereafter. But the close association of the two families throughout their whole lives is illustrated by the fact that Skene, one of Scott's most constant visitors and firmest friends, was married to a sister of Forbes. Skene and his wife were continually at Ashestiel and Abbotsford, so Greenmantle must have heard a good deal of Walter and of his wife and family, and no doubt Skene carried news of his relatives to the Scotts.

Williamina died in 1810 at the age of thirty-nine, after thirteen years of wedded life.

When she died her husband withdrew to the country and gave himself up to the education and career of their children. He saw little society, but was a staunch friend and of high heart in all his ways and thoughts. Of him Scott never spoke but with praise.

In 1793, at St. Andrews, Scott had cut Williamina's name in Runic characters on the turf at the castle gate. Thirty-four years later when sitting on a gravestone there, because his rheumatism would not let him climb St. Regulus with the rest of the party, he asked himself why the recollection of a trifle like that should still agitate his heart. In November of the same year, when Greenmantle and Charlotte were both dead, when Forbes was in his last illness, and when Scott's health was breaking, Mrs. Skene brought him a letter from " one who had been in former happy days no stranger to him." It was from Lady Jane Stuart, and it contained a request. She had in her possession an album that had apparently belonged to Greenmantle, and in this album were some ballads in Scott's handwriting which she desired permission for a friend to print. His reply is not available, but Lady Jane's second letter is, with Scott's reference to it.

" When I came home, a surprise amounting to a shock reached me in another letter from Lady Jane Stuart. Methinks this explains the gloom which hung about me yesterday. I own that the recurrence to these matters seems like a summons to the grave. It fascinates me. I ought perhaps to have stopped it at once, but I have not nerve to do so. Alas ! alas ! But why alas ? Humana perpessi sumus."

Lady Jane said in her letter that she would send him her daughter's manuscript book as a sacred and secret treasure could she but know that he would take it, as she gave it, without a drawback or misconstruction of her intention. The meaning of this I am unfortunate enough not to comprehend.

Then: " Were I to lay open my heart (of which you know little indeed) you would find how it has and ever shall be warm toward you. My age "—she was well over seventy—" encourages me and I have longed to tell you. Not the mother who bore you followed you more anxiously (though secretly) with her blessing than I. Age has its tales to tell and sorrows to unfold." At this time he was staying at 6 Shandwick Place, and Lady Jane stayed near by. Accordingly he went with Mrs. Skene to see her and found her very affectionate. He went to see her again a few days afterwards and they discussed Greenmantle and all about her for hours. Scott came home and shed tears all night after the first visit, but after the second visit he felt that he had indulged himself too far. The old lady had sentimentally enjoyed herself, but she preserved more sorrow than he had. Her daughter had been cut off in early maturity, but Scott's share in her had been merely a youthful dream. " To me these things are now matter of calm and solemn recollection, never to be forgotten, yet scarce to be remembered with pain."

CHAPTER V

LADY SCOTT OF ABBOTSFORD

In July 1797, about nine months after Scott had definitely heard from Greenmantle's own lips that she was going to marry Forbes, he went on tour in England, beginning with the Lakes, and hoping to turn homeward only after he should have explored Wales. His brother the soldier, John, and Adam Fergusson, still in a law office but hankering after the Army too, accompanied him, and all three had their own horses, for there were no trains.

His father had begun to fail, and no doubt he looked forward to his inheritance. The more ill and irritable old Walter became, the less pleasure Scott had in life at home. His friends were marrying and leading lives of joyous happiness, entertaining each other, independent, able to be alone when they desired, and experiencing perhaps the wonderful, poignant sympathies of fatherhood. Walter was a young man of infinite nerve, and throughout his whole life he had the utmost contempt for any considerations of economy or restraint that were based on lack of cash. So, provided he could get a wife with some means, the fact that he had earned only £144, 10s. in the past year was not likely to keep him from thoughts of marriage; besides, when he did make up his mind to marry he asked his father for an allowance. There is not a shadow of a doubt too that, as he had shown Greenmantle's husband daily for months past that his spirits were not abashed by his rejection, he was more than willing to demonstrate to herself that there were other girls in the world.

There are two accounts of Charlotte Charpentier's history and of Scott's meeting with her at Gilsland. Lockhart says that Scott, riding one day with Adam, took some interest in a girl on horseback and was pleased when he ascertained that she was staying at the boarding-house where he had put up. There was a ball that evening, and Fergusson and he went in uniform. They paid some attention to the young lady, and Scott had the pleasure of taking her in to supper.

She was slender and quick in her movements, lively and pleasant, of an olive complexion, with thick raven hair ; and though not a beauty she was very attractive. She was just twenty-one, a French Protestant girl whose parents had fled from the Revolution to London, where they had kindly friends in M. Dumergue, dentist to the King, and in his sisters. Lord Downshire too had been an old friend, and when Charlotte's parents died he had become her guardian.

Lord Downshire had got Charlotte's only brother a post in India, where he was doing so well that he could afford to send his sister £500 a year. Charlotte was travelling for pleasure with her former governess, Miss Jane Nicholson, daughter of the Dean of Exeter.

The Reverend George Gilfillan of Dundee, in an old *Life of Scott* which was pervaded by a peculiar callousness and by no other quality whatsoever, gave another account, but he stated neither his source nor his evidence for it, and I have not traced any. According to the reverend gentleman, Madame Charpentier did not flee from the horrors of the Revolution, but fled from her husband to the Marquis of Downshire. The Marquis, when jobbing young Charles Charpentier into a lucrative post in India, stipulated that the young man should remit £200 a year of his income for the support of his sister. Worst of all, he alleges that Charlotte had already formed an attachment to a young man whose position and prospects were not satisfactory. Accordingly the careful Marquis had sent her down to the house of a pillar of the Church, the Dean of Carlisle, in order to keep her out of her lover's way, and the Dean had taken her on holiday with his family to Gilsland. The Dean's party as newcomers sat at the foot of the hotel table, and young Scott, riding on his way to Wales, sat beside them. The Dean's wife asked him if he knew another Scot, a major of her acquaintance. Walter did, and he found this introduction a pleasant opportunity of seeing more of the dark girl who was with the Dean's family. Mrs. Dean invited him to tea in her private sitting-room, and though at the moment Walter's horse had been ordered to the door to take him away—he stayed. He remained at Gilsland as long as his new friends did, and was growing so obviously in love that Mrs. Dean asked him to go to Carlisle and stay with them. He went, and was an accepted lover in a few weeks.

The dates are a trifle uncertain, but it is quite certain that after an acquaintance of perhaps one week and at most four weeks Scott had asked Charlotte to marry him.

In late August or early September he wrote telling his mother that he had been accepted, subject to Lord Down-shire's consent : he was pathetically anxious that his mother should not think him flighty after his recent experience, but justified himself in making up his mind so soon because he had seen so much of Miss Charpentier. In this letter he twice asked his mother's advice, which is the way of indulged sons after they have done what they desire to do. " Send me your opinion, your advice, and above all your blessing," he wrote, with his own endearing way of assuming that it was all right. Brother John went home before him to carry the great news, and to give their mother all the descriptions.

On 30th September Scott was back in Jedburgh on business, spent a convivial evening with Shortreed, drinking Miss Charpentier's health and " raving about her till one in the morning."

There was nothing romantic about Scott, except his iron will, his passion for planting, and his healthy story-telling life. In matters of marriage he had not an atom of romance. I am convinced that Greenmantle would never have inspired him with youthful passion had she been poor and nameless. The story of Walter's courtship and marriage is not romantic, in spite of the sentimental Shortreed's interpretation.

One of Charlotte's first letters to him is full of fine fun and of fear—fear that reveals an attitude somewhat less fervent than a lover's :

" Lord Downshire . . . his letter is . . . full of advice, much in the style of your last . . . I don't like to reflect on that subject. I am afraid. It is very awful to think it is for life."

Lord Downshire's consent arrived on 8th October, and Scott dashed down to Carlisle for a week to see if Charlotte would marry him immediately. " Oh, my dear sir, no. You must not think of it *this great while.*"

Meantime he wrote to his aunt, Miss Christian, about Charlotte :

" Hem ! Hem ! It must come out. I am in a very fair way of being married to a very amiable young woman with whom I formed an attachment in the course of my tour. . . . I may give you a hint that there is no romance in her composition. . . . She is not a beauty by any means, but her person and face are very engaging. She is a brunette ; her manners are lively, but when necessary she can be very serious. She was baptized and educated a Protestant of the Church of England."

Much like the description of a purchase, and Charlotte's letters to him are no better :

" Indeed, Mr. Scott, I am by no means pleased with all this writing. . . . I will give you a little hint, that is, not to put so many *must* in your letters ; it is beginning rather too soon," —and then she turns the rebuke prettily off. " You must take care of yourself ; you must think of me."

He was again in Carlisle for a few days at the beginning of November, but had to return for the opening of the Court of Session on the twelfth of that month. Charlotte continued to write love-letters to him :

" The settling of our little plans—all looked so much in earnest that I began reflecting more seriously than I generally do, or approve of." " You have made me very *triste* all day. . . . I am glad you don't give up the cavalry, as I love anything that is stylish." " With all my love and those sort of pretty things."

They were married in St. Mary's, Carlisle, on 24th December 1797, about five months after they first met, and they seem to have come straight to Edinburgh. They took rooms in George Street while a house in South Castle Street was being prepared for them. It was not till a year or two afterwards that they moved into the well-known No. 39 in North Castle Street, only a few steps away. Charlotte was anxious about the first fortnight, the inspection of a multitude of relatives and friends, and the entry into absolutely new surroundings which were to be her surroundings for the future.

Many little episodes of those first days struck her as bright and grotesque, and remained in her mind for life. One joke she liked to tell and laugh over. The young married lady sat every afternoon in the drawing-room of the lodging (rented and paid for). But the landlady, with a real Scotch touch, lectured her on the enormity of such a habit and pointed out that the drawing-room should be reserved for special days and occasions. Young Mrs. Scott carried the story to Walter's mother, and got a momentary shock and a joy for ever when she saw that Walter's mother agreed with the landlady.

At the weekly suppers given by the officers of the Light Horse it is to be assumed that Scott and his wife met Green-mantle regularly. As soon as he asked Charlotte to marry him he told her the whole story, and her curiosity must have been intense. He mentioned it in a letter to her as " a period I have often alluded to," but it is probable that the allusions were mostly drawn out by Charlotte, for it was not the kind of story he would be likely to recur to, were it even for the figure it would make him cut in Charlotte's eyes. Yet to conceal it or to make light of it would have been contrary to Walter's upright and explanatory character, and even from motives of prudence he was wise to mention it. Had he ignored it he could not without creating some mistrust in her have sprung it on his bride, and misery would have been her portion when one of the thousand acquaintances of Edinburgh should have dropped the inevitable hint.

She had a pet name for him, but it has never been recorded, and in conversation she referred to him as " Scott." She loved to entertain, and his friends were made welcome by the joyous little wife, who intended to be gay and to be sur-rounded by bright faces. All their lives they were never a week in Edinburgh without going to the theatre, and often they went nightly.

They made up their minds to enjoy life. Walter escaped

from the terrible gloom of George Square, where the focus of the house was the bedroom of an irritable invalid ; and his own houseful of friends, centred round his merry little wife, made heaven for him. When summer came he rented a thatched cottage at Lasswade, with a garden and a field or two. There his wife and he spent the summers of six years, and at the week-ends had the cottage crowded with guests.

From his father, and from his Uncle Robert whose favourite he was, he inherited considerable property. He was made Sheriff of Selkirkshire soon after his marriage, so that at the age of thirty-three, with his wife's income, he had £1000 a year. After receiving his uncle's legacies he got a carriage and a coachman — the steady Peter Mathieson, brother-in-law of Tom Purdie, who was his coachman for life —it was a way Scott had.

Marriage went smoothly with them both, but Scott never made any attempt to show it in a romantic light. To Lady Abercorn he wrote on 21st January 1810, twelve years afterwards :

" I gained no advantage from three years' constancy except . . . experience and some advantage to my conversation and manners. Mrs. Scott's match and mine was of our own making, and proceeded from the most sincere affection on both sides, which has rather increased than diminished during twelve years' marriage. But it was something short of love in all its forms, which I suspect people only feel once in their lives ; folk who have been nearly drowned in bathing rarely venturing a second time out of their depth."

Charlotte's brother settled some stock on her : this produced £200 a year, and as Scott prospered he made his wife a personal allowance of £300 a year. When Charles Charpentier died in 1818 he left the reversion of his fortune to his sister's children, and the estimate sent from India was somewhat exaggerated. The large amount gave Scott great satisfaction, and in Constable's shop he talked of it, but when the actual realisation of assets was completed it was found that the fortune was much less than the sanguine estimate. Then the whole Scott family was vexed to death by the questions that all their friends and acquaintances asked about

Uncle Charles's will. Scott himself was so annoyed that he went about saying he wished he could print all the details above the door for the old wives of Edinburgh to read for themselves.

Abbotsford was open to all kinds of people, and it actually happened, not once or twice, but several times, that persons visited him, were profuse in their expressions of reverence and gratitude till Scott's face was solemn with boredom, and were so engrossed in the great man that they neglected to pay ordinary civility to his wife and children. The great man retained his manners, but could not help whispering in the nearest sympathetic ear, " I would have these gentry understand that, books or no books, I started by being a *gentleman*, and mean to keep up the character."

There are indications that as a housewife Charlotte was careless, though there are no details to demonstrate it. Sir Walter himself in 1826 spoke of " our careless habits " in the matter of food and farm produce. That she did not enter with any kind of enthusiasm into her husband's literary work has sometimes been made a matter of reproach, but it has to be remembered that that was the last thing in the world he would have encouraged her to do. He despised his own novels and lived to feel contempt for his verses. He kept his books from his children, and disliked to converse with any person on earth about them, except in the way of business.

But Lady Scott sat at table and interrupted his jokes, while the Dominie spilt his tea at the Sheriff's exquisite replies to the interruptions. Prosperity changed her, though it had not an atom of effect on the Sheriff. When the crash came in 1826 and he had to announce the bitter news to his wife, he recorded in his journal :

" Lady Scott is incredulous, and persists in cherishing hope where there is no ground for hope."

And again :

" Another person did not afford me all the sympathy I expected, perhaps because I seemed to need little support yet that is not her nature, which is generous and kind."

Perhaps this lack of sympathy was entirely due to ill-health, for already she was suffering greatly from chronic asthma. Realisation of the disaster, however, preyed on her spirits, and she sank under it. In March symptoms of dropsy appeared, and on the 15th of that month, while ill-health confined her to Abbotsford, the dearly loved Edinburgh house at 39 Castle Street was sold and the contents that she had cherished were dissipated to the four winds. On 19th April, Scott had to leave his bedroom to make way for a servant to attend Charlotte. Everybody in the house was overworked, and the arrival of cousin Anne to help to nurse was hailed as a godsend. Lady Scott preserved to the last the pluck that had made her in youth a fearless horsewoman ; she would not speak out about her symptoms. When her husband came into her room she welcomed him with a smile, and invariably said she felt better.

" I admire of all things your laughing philosophy," young Walter had written to her before marriage. It was a stedfast character that underlay the determined light-heartedness of the girl.

On 11th May, Scott had to return to his table at the Court of Session, and on the morning of that day when he saw that his wife was soundly sleeping he did not waken her. On the 15th she died. She was then about fifty or fifty-one.

Her children were very fond of her, and the big soldier Walter is said to have taken his mother's death very much to heart. But it was most calamitous for Scott himself. Erskine, his chief confidant, was gone. Three of his four children had left him on the necessary business of life : the burden of £117,000 of debt was now on his shoulders : he had had some paralytic seizures, and he was in a fearfully nervous state. Yet his great spirit never shrank from its tasks, bitter as they were, and without any joy but the barren satisfaction of obstacles overcome. His remaining six years of life were a fierce battle in which though he was slain he conquered, leaving behind him a record of magnificent courage, of a sense of honour that commands admiration, and of superiority to all the misfortunes of life.

CHAPTER VI

INTERESTING PEOPLE ASSOCIATED WITH SCOTT

It is partly Sir Walter's own vivid descriptions that have made these characters interesting, but many of the people with whom he associated at one time or another are worthy of record. Every one of his intimates may be pictured as a portion of himself, as an illumination of one facet of his own character, kindling in him a light finer than the illumination itself. In peer and peasant he found delight : the death of the Duke of Buccleuch was to him a calamity the like of which in his lifetime he suffered few—the death of his own father was a trifle in comparison—and the sudden death of his dearest Tom Purdie was a calamity even greater. In John Ballantyne, the schemer, mimic, drinker, jockey and so forth, he delighted ; and in Will Erskine, who never mounted a horse and could not fire a gun, whose eyes filled with tears on the smallest of provocations, he had the deepest confidences of his life.

The exquisite flavour of Scotchness about dozens of the people of his time is to be found nowhere else, not even in Sir Walter's own novels. There was the old doctor of divinity who declared at the tea-table of Sandyknowe that he might as well talk in the mouth of the cannon as where " that child " was. The marvellous child of three years old meantime wandered about the room reciting *Hardyknute,* an egregious imitation of a ballad. At twenty-five the whilom child visited the old man of ninety, emaciated to bones, told by his doctors he could only last a fortnight, and calmly but busily writing a history. Possibly with an instinctive notion of revenge he proceeded to read large portions of what he had written, and after a time Walter, seeing the effort it was, said he should spare himself.

" What matter ? " replied the doctor. " I have a fortnight to live, and any over-exertion can only make the difference of a day or two."

Another type of the Scot at his dourest was Sir Walter's uncle Thomas Scott on his death-bed. Dosed with tonics or sedatives, possibly at the entreaties of his womenfolk, he retained the gruesome mouthfuls, sank back in his bed and carefully spat them into his handkerchiefs.

" I have lived all my life without taking doctors' drugs, and I want to die without taking them."

" Doctors' drugs " and " doctors' bottles " are epithets that may be heard in tones of contempt from the disillusioned victims in every village of Scotland to this day.

Presbyterianism in Scott's youth, and before it, was very rigid, and accordingly it is to be assumed that the dandy of the following story was an Episcopalian. Sir Matthew Riddell used to feel warm in church, so he often took off his wig, washed his head in the christening font, and dried it with his handkerchief. The authority for this story is old Mackenzie, author of *The Man of Feeling*, and a great friend of Scott's.

Another man, of as terrific a pluck, that fortunately took other directions, was old James Ferrier, one of Scott's fellow-Clerks of Session, and father of Miss Ferrier the novelist. He retired in 1825 or so, at the age of eighty-one, and as he suffered from giddiness his daughter insisted on accompanying him everywhere and watching him like a hawk. His chief pleasure in life was to evade her and go off for a walk by himself. On one of these escapes he took a turn of giddiness, fell against a lamp-post, cut himself badly and was carried home.

" This," said the old man of eighty-one as he bled, " was the luckiest thing that could have happened, for bleeding is exactly the cure for my giddiness."

The courage of these instances is matched by the courtesy of Philip Anstruther, a light-hearted sailor and a friend of Scott's. Once, wanting money, he drew on his father, who wrote an angry letter when he discovered Philip's defalcation. Philip, who had embezzled the old man's money, wrote back that if his father did not know how to write like a gentleman he did not desire any more of his correspondence.

Mr. Plummer of Middlestead, the Sheriff of Selkirkshire who was the immediate predecessor of Scott, gathered a fine library which was in possession of three maiden sisters when Scott entered into his sheriffdom. Scott was eager to investigate the library and took the precaution of leaving big Camp at home lest he should dirty the carpets of the ladies, but took with him some greyhounds as a gentle hint that hare soup might be forthcoming in due season. This is a good illustration of the countryside Scott lived in. There were no shops, no vans, no means of ordering anything except at a fortnight's notice. I do not know whether or not Sheriff Plummer died before his time, but he deserved to. He said that a walk from the parlour to the garden once a day was sufficient exercise for any rational being, and that no one but a fool or a fox-hunter would take more.

It was a fateful day for the readers of books when old Alexander Stewart of Invernahyle, a Jacobite who had fought in the '45, walked into the elder Walter Scott's office or perhaps came to dinner in George Square, and fairly fascinated young Walter. The lad hung on his words with eager pleasure, and delighted the old man with his boyish enthusiasm, his interest in the Jacobite cause, and his intelligence. He was invited to Invernahyle, and thither Walter went in the summer in which he was sixteen.

In the beautiful sunshine, that is never so sweet in July or August as among the heather, he passed into the Highlands on his pony, alone : a perilous adventure at that time for any but those joyous souls who are on friendly terms with everything that lives, and are favoured of Fortune as well. Jogging along on the last stage of his journey he came to a bleak height overlooking a little tower, and beheld two striking groups of people. Half-asleep on the heather beside him lay a number of tartan-clad men : Invernahyle, his three sons, and half a dozen ghillies, with guns and dogs and game lying about them. In the courtyard of the tower below was a company of women loading a cart with manure. The men welcomed young Walter, and all together went down to the tower. Judge Walter's surprise when three of the women loading the manure-cart were introduced to him as Invernahyle's wife and daughters.

The ladies at least were quite without embarrassment, soon went off to dress, and reappeared to entertain him with talk, singing and dancing.

Walter went back to Invernahyle yearly for some time.

Old Stewart was both an ardent soldier and an excellent teller of stories about battles and other affairs. Nothing pleased him better than to tell his yarns, and nothing pleased the creative boy better than to listen. Speaking broadly, it is probable that he got more education from Invernahyle than from all his schoolmasters.

At Ashestiel his chief companion was Lord Somerville, a neighbour. To Somerville belongs the credit of awakening in Scott the joy of a planter of trees or " landscape gardener." He was a fine sylviculturist, and Scott always spoke of him as his instructor. Somerville was not let into the secret of the authorship of the novels, and he took some pleasure in teasing the Sheriff on the subject. On the boat at Cauldshiels that accommodated fishers and view-hunters he painted the name " Search No. 2," with only too plain an allusion to Search No. 1 in chapter xxiv. of *The Antiquary*. Probably the name of the *Search* was bestowed on the boat because it was borrowed by all and sundry, while the owner sought for it in vain.

A very different facet of Scott was the earnest Johnnie Bower, keeper of Melrose Abbey. Johnnie took Melrose Abbey and Scott's poetry about it equally seriously, and when tourists turned up on moonless nights in obedience to Scott's doggerel,

> " If thou wouldst view fair Melrose aright
>   Go visit it by the pale moonlight,"

Johnnie was ready for them. He had a big tallow-candle on the end of a long stick : he gave them romantic " views " of the abbey, and triumphantly pointed out that he could illuminate the north " view " and the moon could not.

" He'll come here sometimes wi' great folks in his company, and the first I'll know of it is hearing his voice call out ' Johnnie ! Johnnie Bower ! ' and when I go out I'm sure to be greeted wi' a joke or a pleasant word. He'll stand and crack and lauch wi' me just like an auld wife—and to think that o' a man that has such an awfu' knowledge o' history ! "

Johnnie wore a tile, a blue coat with brass buttons, and a red waistcoat. In those garments he was imposing in life, and when he took over the post of caretaker he stipulated that his death also was to be made imposing by an obituary notice from the Sheriff's pen.

Johnnie touches the character of the Sheriff with one grotesque notion that could have originated in no quarter but the Sheriff's own whimsical head. Johnnie harped so much on " the view " of this piece of architecture that he got the length of requiring his tourists, old and young, male and female, to stand off a bit, bend down and " view " the ruin through their own legs.

" It gives ye quite a new view o't," he would say. " It's surprisin'."

He was disappointed that ladies would seldom obey his instructions, and preferred to look through their arm ; but it is pleasant to realise that most of the peerage of that generation, urged on by Scott's romantic poetry, doubled themselves up and looked through their legs at Melrose Abbey to get another " view " of it.

I have not a shadow of doubt that Johnnie derived this notion from a joke of the Sheriff's. Nobody knew better than he how inappropriate is sentimental verse to the cold, virgin art of architecture. Nobody could joke about romantic interpretations better than he. " Damn it, Tom ; don't be poetical," was often in his mouth, and he kept his own romantic verse from his children as though it were an unclean thing. Johnnie's harping on " the view " undoubtedly evoked this suggestion from the Sheriff.

When Will Clerk, son of John Clerk of Eldin, and nephew of a baronet, made his acquaintance at the Scots Law Class, Will was shocked at Walter's glazed corduroy breeches that the stick had rubbed shabby. Before he spoke to his fellow-student he said that Scott looked like a hautboy-player, because of the soft continual movement of the upper lip that was characteristic of him throughout life. The seventeen-year-old boys took to each other with great joy, and Will introduced Scott to many families of the minor aristocracy as a " man " of marvellous memory and deep reading. In introducing him to society Clerk probably did a great deal to develop Scott's natural bent and natural ambition.

Will and he passed their examinations together and put on the advocate's gown on the same day, 11th July 1792. They were always together at that time, for Will was Darsie Latimer of *Redgauntlet*. He was a great quoter of verse and prose, and was renowned for the aptness and variety of his quotations. He was also a conversationalist, and prided himself on impressing everybody; but he got at least one staggerer in the conversational line. Once in a stage-coach he tried to talk to another man, but time and again got nothing but grunts for his pains. At length, as the journey was long and there was no other company, he expostulated:

" I have talked to you, my friend, on all the ordinary subjects—literature, farming, merchandise, gaming, game laws, horse-racing, suits-at-law, politics, swindling, blasphemy and philosophy—is there any one subject that you will favour me by opening upon ? "

The man grinned.

" Sir," said he, " can you say anything clever about *bend leather* ? "

In old age Scott recorded that he had never met a man of greater powers or of more complete information on all desirable subjects than Will. He remained a bachelor and so did not entertain often, but his dinners were much enjoyed when he gave them. He usually depended on some gourmand such as Adam Fergusson to do the ordering, and had the endearing quality of showing himself anxious that his evening should be a pleasant one for everybody. Probably at his own dinners he put off the habit of arguing his friends to a standstill. He was rather inclined to pursue a conversation till he secured a conviction, for he was a lawyer.

R. P. Gillies, another advocate, deserves honourable mention. Scott liked him and did a good deal to assist him after he had run through a fortune : apparently his practice was not worth talking about.

At the request of Scott, Constable commissioned Gillies to do some translations from German. There was always some whim in Gillies's head, and at that time the whim was to write, not with pen or pencil on foolscap, but with a paint-brush on huge sheets of cartridge paper.   In due time the MS. of the translations arrived at Constable's publishing house in two bales and on the backs of lorrymen.   Constable declined to look at it, no doubt thinking that since the translator was mad the translations would be madder.

Daniel Terry

In January 1810 Mrs. Scott took a party of thirty friends into one small box of Henry Siddons's Edinburgh theatre at the first night's performance of *The Family Legend*, by Joanna Baillie.   Scott himself went that night and the next night, and was much struck by the actor who did the Earl of Argyle. To this actor, Dan Terry, he was introduced by the Ballantynes, who were both theatre-mad and both admirers and companions of Terry, and Scott was surprised to find him an educated man and "a virtuoso like himself," as he had said of Mrs. Cockburn when he was six.   Terry had been trained as an architect ;   he was a rare companion, could cap Sir Walter's quotations from any of the English dramatists, and loved old armour, old furniture and old nicknackets with as much passion as Scott and with more judgment than he.

But above and beyond all these points Terry staggered the world and Scott by copying the poet (not yet the novelist) in all he said, looked and wrote.   He came from Bath, but he had not been many times at Ashestiel and Castle Street before he had the Sheriff's very tone and very accent, and was taken for a Border Scot by all who knew no better.   His face was small and dark and alert, but he cultivated his own tiny black threads of eyebrows till he was perfect in the deep-set droop of Scott's shaggy, overhanging brows.   He imitated Scott's handwriting so cleverly and so habitually that the Sheriff used to declare that if he were called on to swear to any document that looked like his own penmanship he could only say that it was his—or Terry's.

He had no limp, and so could hardly imitate the Sheriff's walk.   But on one occasion the two comedians Charles Mathews and Terry were flung out of a gig together, and, though Terry escaped, Mathews was laid up with injuries that made him limp for ever after.

" Dooms, Dauniel," said Charlie when he met Dan for the first time after the accident, " what a pity it wasna *your* luck to get the game leg. Your Sheriff would hae been complete then."

Terry imitated Scott, and Mathews sent them all into roars by caricaturing Terry's imitation. It is scenes like those of which we regret the absolute destruction : the innocent hero-worship of a capable and pliant spirit ; and more innocent fun of the whole thing, done by a master before many men good at a hundred things.

Terry was one of the few to whose reading aloud the Sheriff took pleasure in listening. He was also much on the scene when Abbotsford was in its first plan, rode over with the Sheriff from Ashestiel, and advised him daily for some weeks about the planning of the house and the development of the grounds, as his architectural training enabled him to do.

In 1812 Terry established himself in London, but he returned to Edinburgh nearly every year, and was always much in Scott's company while in Scotland. Scott wrote him regularly, and made him a kind of London agent to procure articles of vertu, rare books and other items. He turned over his novels regularly to Terry for dramatisation, and himself did a good deal of the stage copy of *Guy Mannering* and probably of others.

At first Terry played in the Haymarket, but in about a year's time he got an engagement for three years at Covent Garden at £650 a year. He became stage-manager of the Haymarket in 1818, in 1825 joined Frederick Yates as lessee and manager of the Adelphi Theatre, and applied to James Ballantyne and Scott for backing. Scott became his surety for £1250 and Ballantyne for £500, though Sir Walter was pretty certain that Terry was not a good business man and was not likely to make the undertaking a success. He was right, for in one short year Terry failed, and Sir Walter not only lost his £1250 but had to pay up Ballantyne's £500.

To London he had carried his wife, who was a daughter of Nasmyth the painter, and who herself painted and drew with

4

ability. When a son was born he could think of just one name for him—Walter. When the theatre failed in 1826 Terry at first fled to Boulogne, but returned to face the footlights. The bankruptcy broke up his home, and little Walter was sent to Edinburgh to his grandfather's house, while Sir Walter paid for his schooling at the Edinburgh Academy.

The failure spoilt Terry's health as well as his prospects : he appears to have had a shock, and lingered till 22nd June 1829. His widow married Mr. Charles Richardson of Tulse Hill, " the author of the well-known Dictionary of the English Language, etc.," a change indeed from the comedian-architect-virtuoso.

Scott and his friends were inveterate nicknamers. He rejoiced in his own designations of " The Shirra " and " The Duke of Darnick." He had weird names for the Ballantynes, and gave several to Constable. The meanest labourer on his estate and the smallest item in the printing-house was not safe from the Sheriff's epithets, which were mostly but not always kindly. Either he or some other of " the gang " named Terry " The Grinder," after a song of that name that he sang, and because of the harsh notes of his voice when he spoke or sang in a low key. The art of turning the novels into plays was " terryfication," another invention of Sir Walter's.

WILL ERSKINE

There was only one man whom Scott ever placed reliance on and was fond of, who was not an outdoor man and a handy man at sports and exercises ; and that man, William Erskine, was as divergent from Scott's type as he could possibly be. He was the son of an Episcopalian minister in Perthshire, was educated in Glasgow, knew something of Latin, encouraged and helped Scott in his early studies of German, with the help of his sister (Mary Ann) entertained him while he was yet a bachelor, and clung to Scott in such a self-sacrificing way as no other man except Tom Purdie did.

He was a small man with a feeble body, unhappy on horseback, especially at fords, horrified at the notion of handling a gun, shuddering at the sight of a party equipped for the hunt and reserving a particular detestation for fishermen. His features were small and shapely, his eyes a soft brown, his cheeks flushed and sensitive, and he had as delicate a spirit. A beautiful landscape or a fine strain of music sent tears rolling down his cheeks. It is probable that he took his share of wine, but as he was a constant user of snuff it may be assumed that he did not smoke. This was the chosen confidant of Walter Scott, the six-footer, the convivial, the iron of heart, the sportsman.

He read chiefly to supply Scott with facts and suggestions, for he had the gift of extracting living matter from dry books. And if he assisted the Sheriff, there is no doubt that the Sheriff's burly esteem and encouragement were of great help to the sensitive spirit of Erskine. They were perfectly confident in each other. When in 1805 Scott set himself up as a partner in the printing business of James Ballantyne & Co. he told Erskine, but not another soul. Early in his literary life Scott habitually consulted Erskine when in doubt about any matter large or small. It was to him that the first six or seven chapters of *Waverley* were submitted in 1805, and he told Scott that they were not good enough to publish ; this of course was owing to the well-known dulness of those opening chapters. Time and again that part of the shrewd public that prided itself on being in the know attributed Scott's verse as well as his prose to Erskine, and Will sunned himself in many a good joke of the kind.

He had a passion for his books, and lending them gave him nearly as much pain as the drawing of teeth. He kept his library locked, entertained visitors in other rooms lest they should borrow his volumes, and to make assurance doubly sure he provided his bookcases with closed fronts, so that if cadgers did gain admittance to his sacred chamber they should behold nothing of his treasures.

Like Scott he was an advocate, and Scott's friendly nickname for him was " The Counsellor." In due time he also got a sheriffdom, that of Orkney and Shetland, but for a long time he did not arrive at eminence in his profession. He considered that his powerful friends and connections (Mary Ann had married a Lord Advocate) ought to have jobbed him on farther, and he grew somewhat snappish both to the lords on the bench in public and about the leaders of the Tory party in private. These things Scott eventually took much to heart, and he persuaded Lord Advocate Rae to get Erskine promoted to the Bench. He took his seat in January 1822, as Lord Kinnedder.

His constitution, however, had already been shaken, and the duties of a judge, which appear expressly devised to diminish exertion of the mind and to prolong life, exhausted his sensitive body. While he was unwell, some one sent about a foul lie that he was conducting an intrigue. The rumour reached him and preyed on his innocent mind : it finished what probably was not in any case destined long to survive, the sensitive, shrinking body of as fresh a soul as ever inhabited the fabric of man. He died just on the first day of the king's visit to Edinburgh. Scott had sat long and often by his bedside, and from there and from the funeral had to plunge with a sore heart into the merry dinners and banquets that were not complete without Sir Walter. Erskine could not rid himself of the notion that his character had been degraded in the eyes of the public, and no argument relieved his worry. If Scott had not been busy night and day with preparations for the king's visit, and if he had been available continually to sustain his friend's spirit, the issue might have been different ; but even this is doubtful, for he had been ailing before.

THE ETTRICK SHEPHERD

James Hogg served for ten years on the farm of Blackhouse, with the Laidlaws, and it was Willie Laidlaw who introduced him to Scott. Hogg was as young, as enthusiastic and as whimsical as the Sheriff himself, and he was continually so absurd that when they were together he kept Scott in one long outburst of laughter. Scott used to say that nothing he ever saw on the stage, nor even the private extravagances of Mathews, Terry or John Ballantyne, approached the fun of Hogg's native innocence.

He taught himself to write by copying letters from a printed book : he was not long of making songs, and he inherited from his mother a keen love of the Border ballads, for the old dame had them by heart, and debated, or rather denounced, various readings of them to the Sheriff himself.

On a remote hillside on a fine summer day the herdboy told Hogg that he was wanted.

" Wha wants me ? " asked the Shepherd.

" I think it's the Shirra and some o' his gang."

Respect for the myrmidons of the law was never strong on the Borders. Hogg went down to see this Sheriff, a young man of thirty, and to begin a lifelong friendship with him. The shepherd was in his way a striking figure too. Short, rather thick-set, extremely active to the day of his death, wide-nostrilled, and with a particularly impudent expression of face that was as truthful as it was plain, he had at the same time such a jolly round countenance and such an infectious laugh that everybody was delighted with him. And when he associated with the Sheriff's friends he could hold his own. He sang capitally and played the violin ; his absurdities carried off his eternal impudence ; he had no shyness, could preside at dinner as well as any town councillor, and never made the mistake of letting anybody else do the talking.

Scott told him about his projects of publishing, and these gave Hogg the notion of publishing his own songs and stories ; accordingly the next time he was in Edinburgh with a flock of sheep he got a publisher to print his ballads, but they were not a success. Not long afterwards, when Scott had published his third volume of the *Minstrelsy*, Hogg thought that Scott's own *Imitations of the Ancients* were not much good, and he wrote some imitative ballads to show how the thing ought to be done. These he sent to Scott, who was struck by them, and when he was next in Edinburgh and called at Castle Street he was asked to stay to dinner.

When Hogg entered the drawing-room Mrs. Scott was lying on a sofa. The Shepherd was introduced, made his bow and stretched himself on the other sofa, believing, as he afterwards explained, that he could not do wrong if he copied the lady of the house. He was dressed like any other shepherd and his hands were stained with sheep-dip. The party included Laidlaw and some of Hogg's admirers, so he felt at home, dined heartily, drank well, told his stories, sang his songs and enjoyed himself immensely. As the evening wore on he grew familiar : from " Mr. Scott " he came down to " Shirra," then to " Scott," " Walter," and " Wattie," till at supper the whole company went into a roar when he addressed Mrs. Scott as " Charlotte." He wrote the next day to apologise for having been too free ; began his letter " Dear Mr. Scott," finished it with " dear Walter," and illumined his character by mentioning that he was everlastingly promising copies of his verses with no intention of furnishing them. He took the occasion to ask Scott to put his name to a biographic introduction that was to be written by Hogg himself.

He was an unfortunate dog. Listen to Scott the raconteur putting Hogg's career in a nutshell :

" There is an old saying of the seamen—' every man is not born to be a boatswain.' Something of this vile influence gleamed in at the cottage window when poor Hogg first came squeaking into the world. All that he made by his original book he ventured on a flock of sheep to drive into the Highlands to a farm he had taken there but of which he could not get possession, so that all the stock was ruined and sold to disadvantage. Then he tried another farm which proved too dear, so that he fairly broke upon it. Then he put forth divers publications which had little sale and brought him accordingly few pence, though some praise. Then came *The Queen's Wake*, by which he might and ought to have made from £100 to £200, for there were, I think, three editions, when lo ! his bookseller turned bankrupt and paid him never a penny."

Scott was continually endeavouring to assist him, and the more Scott tried the more embarrassing grew Hogg's demands. He wanted to publish for his own benefit a volume to which each of the other poets of his time was to contribute a poem. He applied to Scott and Byron who both refused, and Scott's letter of refusal so annoyed Hogg that he wrote back accusing him of jealousy. Either on this occasion or on a similar one he began a letter to Scott " Damned Sir " and ended " Believe me, Sir, yours with disgust." For a while afterwards they neither wrote nor spoke, till Hogg was struck down with illness in Edinburgh. Scott heard of this and told a friend of Hogg's to employ a good medical man at his expense, but to say nothing of this to the patient. When the Shepherd recovered, however, he learnt of Scott's kindness and wrote humbly enough asking for a reconciliation. The Sheriff replied briefly, telling him to come to breakfast next morning, and think no more about it.

Hardly were they friends, however, before the outrageous Hogg took offence again, though this time without showing it openly. After a great football match at Carterhaugh several guests adjourned to dinner with the Duke of Buccleuch. Hogg danced down at a particular table, and the Sheriff took him by the arm and carried him to an inferior place, namely between Walter Scott and the laird of Harden. " I am convinced he was sore afraid of my getting to be too great a favourite among the young ladies of Buccleuch," wrote Hogg in one of his auto-biographies. But Scott had merely prevented him from sitting at the side table reserved for the children.

There was a certain clumsiness of importunity about Hogg that beat all other requesters hollow. When he got some reputation as a poet he dunned Scott and Scott's powerful friends to get him a commission in the Militia, a job in the Excise, and then a farm ; ultimately the Duke of Buccleuch gave him " the gratuitous liferent " of Altrive, a small farm in the Vale of Yarrow. Here, instead of playing the farmer, he kept nearly as much of a free hotel for admirers as Scott kept at Abbotsford, and for months out of every year he was to be found in Edinburgh, attending to his pleasures.

When he dedicated *The Forest Minstrel* to Lady Dalkeith, who afterwards became Duchess of Buccleuch, she sent him a hundred guineas. She was fond of him and of his bright rustic ways, and it is recorded that once when both were staying at Abbotsford she sent a messenger to find him for a game at cards. This summons from the Duchess found him in the cottage of his brother, the shepherd of Abbotsford, where he had looked in for an hour.

Scott had a keen enough sense of biography to keep Hogg's letters, but Hogg was incapable of keeping anything, and all Scott's letters to him are lost.

He married in 1819 when he was over forty, and forthwith got a larger farm on the Buccleuch estate, but misfortune followed him there too.   Accordingly when Scott had arranged places for himself and Hogg in Westminster Abbey from which to see the coronation, and hoped that Hogg would make a pension out of it, the Shepherd thought that he ought to go to the Border fair at St. Boswells Green, lest the other farmers should think him a gadabout.

One of Hogg's finest days was the day the *Edinburgh Review* published a paper abusing his two volumes of *Jacobite Relics* but praising as a fine old Jacobite strain some verses of Hogg's own called Donald Magillavry.   Another uproarious day, which was yearly repeated, was the annual dinner of the Gala master-weavers.   Scott usually went as principal guest, and Hogg was invariably there.   It must have been an imposing sight when John of Skye the piper, and the weavers with their banners, met the carriage of Sir Walter and his family at the ford, turned, and escorted them to the inn.

At another yearly festival Hogg was the chief figure.   When Innerleithen became famous as St. Ronan's, a club of Bowmen of the Border, who dressed in a uniform of green, with broad blue bonnets, set up annual games there.   Hogg was their Captain, and Scott wore the uniform of a member. Even when he was about sixty Hogg astonished many of the young men by carrying off prizes regularly.   In the evening he presided at dinner, with Scott and Sir Adam Fergusson close by.

In the company of poets Hogg had a certain uneasiness that betrayed itself by assertiveness.   He brought another rhymester to Scott once, and referred to "huz Tevidale poets." In company with Wordsworth and De Quincey he spoke blithely of the meeting of "the poets," and De Quincey poisoned him by telling him afterwards that Wordsworth had whispered to him, "Poets! What does the fellow mean ? Where are the *poets* ? "   Like the rest of us he did not know whether to believe De Quincey or not.   He discussed with Sir Walter one " Muir," an Irish warbler, and rather deprecated his verses as "owre sweet ; for they're sweeter than mine, and mine are just richt."

He died on 21st November 1835.

ARCHIBALD CONSTABLE

Constable was born in Carnbee, Fife, in 1774, two and a half years after the birth of Scott. He was so impressed by the good clothes of the village bookseller and stationer that he asked his father, a factor, to apprentice him to the trade, and at fourteen he was apprenticed to a publisher in Edinburgh. He served there seven years, grew up with a beautiful face, a fine figure, a brain for business second to none, wit and humour not far inferior to Sir Walter's own, a knowledge of books which Scott found useful and which, as shown in his correspondence, was greatly superior to that of the average professor of English. He was the most generous of publishers : he developed the trade in books more than any other single man ever did. Prosperity, however, made him fat, and he died of dropsy at fifty-three. But if he died young he matured young. He was a publisher on his own account at twenty-one, and while he was only twenty he married Mary Willison, daughter of a printer, with whom he had been in love at a distance " for several years." No doubt it was the cash and connection of Mary's father that made things easy for the young publisher.

He was very imposing, very ready of speech, and a master of his calling. He believed that he knew more about publishing books than anybody else did, and probably this was true. He loved a good book for its binding and material as well as for its contents, and liked to make his friends blindfold him to test whether he could tell every rare book in his large library by touch. Once when they put a strange rarity into his hands he said he must have overestimated the strength of his memory, for he did not know that one. His judgment of popular taste was perfect : he had an instinct for successes and failures, and he loved to be liberal. His chief nickname was " The Crafty," but he liked to be called " The Czar " and he was as inveterate a nicknamer as Scott.

At some time or other Constable became publisher of the *Edinburgh Review*, and in 1812 he acquired the copyright of the *Encyclopædia Britannica*, which was apparently his best-paying publication, but everything he published prospered. He had some trouble in convincing the other publishers that advertising was profitable, but he was one of the earliest to realise that it was.

Some years after setting up as a publisher he took as partner a man Hunter, a laird and a trial to everybody, including his own father who once threatened to cut him off. Hunter was stupid enough to insist that when Scott undertook to edit for his firm an edition of Swift he was not to undertake any other literary work. Two jobs at a time, of course, were Sir Walter's minimum, and a necessity if he was to do anything at all, and besides that he was not going to take dictation from any Lothian laird. So from 1808 till 1810, when Hunter retired, Scott would have nothing to do with Constable & Co. Constable was greatly vexed when Scott forsook him. He is said to have stamped on the ground in a high and mighty way he had and to have smiled bitterly : " Aye, there is such a thing as rearing the oak till it can support itself."

Scott set up John Ballantyne with the express purpose of cutting Constable out. It says much for Constable's magnanimity that when Hunter retired he immediately made advances to Scott, and they resumed their close acquaintance. For John Ballantyne Constable had some liking, and too much contempt to be in the least troubled by his antics as a publisher.

Early in Constable's career there was a crisis in the publishing business, one of many, and some of his fellow-publishers went to jail as debtors. From jail they issued invitations to dinner (to be brought in at Constable's expense), but the warning was lost on the sanguine young man. He kept his business going on an interchange of bills. Nothing was ever bought or paid for in cash. No publisher of that time had the least notion of his financial standing. If he had a solid basis of cash in land or property—good : if not, the momentary convenience of banks might ruin him.

He too wanted an estate and the name of founding a family. He bought the estate of Balniel in Fife.

And so strangely infatuated were both Scott and he in the matter of their debts and properties that in May 1825, just when the earth was beginning to shake beneath their feet, Constable came to Abbotsford to propound a revolution in cheap issues. He flourished the income-tax return, and pointed out that though hair-powder had gone out of fashion, the tax on it (for servants) at a guinea a wig showed more people taxed for it than any estimate he could make of the purchasers of books. He went on in a half-inspired fashion about armorial bearings, hunters, racers and four-wheeled carriages, convinced Scott (and prophesied truly as we now see) that bookselling and cheap issues were in their infancy. James Ballantyne sat by, open-mouthed and dumb with astonishment. Scott and Constable drove round by Smailholm and Dryburgh, and the whole burden of their talk was the new scheme of publishing, which they were certain was going to make both of them richer than ever.

Constable's health began to break in 1821, and he resided in England for two or three years. On 31st May 1822, after he began to go about, he went up to London and collected gifts for his friends. All in a heap he got for Sir Walter (1) a picture, supposed to be of James IV.; (2) two large carved chairs in boxwood from the Borghese Palace ; (3) a slab of mosaic which he thought suitable for a hearthstone but of which the Scotts made a table-top. The next year Scott made Constable a better gift, when he gave him all the MSS. of the Waverley Novels. At that time Scott acknowledged that Constable had richly endowed his library at Abbotsford, for he was in youth and age an eager collector of rare books and manuscripts. He also gave Sir Walter a complete edition of the Variorum Classics in 128 volumes, " the most splendid present, as I sincerely believe, which ever an author received from a bookseller."

Scott wanted to call his novel about Tressilian and Amy Robsart by the name of *Cumnor Hall*, but Constable persuaded him to name it *Kenilworth*. His partner related that once he supplied Scott with a list of books and papers that could be consulted for a work to be called *The Armada*, and Scott replied thanking him heartily for the list. Constable then stalked up and down the room shouting out, " By God, I am all but the author of the Waverley Novels." This is a good joke, but it is not true. When Cadell told it he had quarrelled with Constable and had separated from him. It is exactly the fashion in which the other publishers, the Ballantynes and the rest, would use Constable's well-known pride in order to caricature him.   The real ground of this story is that Scott wrote to Constable on 23rd March 1822 :

" They talk of a farmer making two blades of grass grow where one grew before, but you, my good friend, have made a dozen volumes where probably but one would have existed," meaning that by paying as no publisher had ever paid, by getting books circulated as they never had been circulated before, and by encouragement and help, Constable had a real share in the production of them.

Constable in a letter to Cadell shortly afterwards translated this into his own expressions, which probably seemed ridiculous enough to the censorious partner : " For the works of the author of *Waverley* everything that bookseller could do has been done.   I am sometimes half tempted to believe that of these books I am myself all but the author.   You may accuse me of vanity if you please, but this I hold to be true."

Those who had a glance at this letter and did not know what a sound basis it rested on would naturally put it down to Constable's vanity, but he had Scott's own support for his view.   The stalking up and down and the shouting are, of course, merely malicious inventions.

His pride was notorious, but of his despotic rages so often alluded to by Lockhart there is no anecdote nor evidence. He was a man of careless generosity.   He hated to haggle, gave abundant measure rather than present the remotest appearance of meanness, and was not only liberal to a man like Scott but paid his routine workers with generous hand. His generosity on behalf of one of these hacks is pathetic. Dr. Duncan Forbes, who had a medical degree but never got a patient, who had passed through the theological college but never got a kirk, lived on the work he did for Constable, dunned him for money and books and hospitality, and by begging, borrowing and stealing had acquired a very fair library.   But he was notoriously poor, and complained of his poverty to everybody.   He chose to die just after Constable went bankrupt, and the publisher, taking pity lest a pauper's funeral should be the doctor's end, wrote to the lawyer who had taken charge of his small affairs saying that he was at the moment unable to defray the expenses of the funeral but took them upon himself and would pay them in due course.   He received word by return that the doctor had died worth £1500.

These friends of Scott and many more are worthy of the interest or affection of us who come after him, but above them all I admire Constable.   While other publishers were grubbing along, this man, even in youth, had evolved visions of the spread of books among millions who were then entirely uneducated.   While other publishers haggled and pared he delighted and astonished the makers of books with generous payments.   His spirit was as open as his bright, handsome face :   time and again Scott and the Ballantynes played him somewhat less than fair :   they milked him, stipulated that he should cumber his acceptances of Waverley Novels with the unsaleable volumes of their own publishing :   they continually tantalised him, eager and downright as he was.   Scott indeed hardly ever spoke of Constable without some trifle of malice. He sneered at his good looks, at his stoutness, at his generosity. Yet I have never seen any evidence that Constable did other than pay continual homage to Scott :   he was anxious for reconciliation after estrangement ;   he revered Scott's powers, and suffered keenly when any publication of his was not offered to the firm of Constable & Co.

CHAPTER VII

THE PERSONALITY OF SIR WALTER

It is common knowledge that none of Sir Walter's painters succeeded in representing him as he really was. Their desire and their achievement were to lessen the Peak, to transform his large, loose, humorous mouth into a vacuous Cupid's bow, to conceal the fact that his nose was rather pug, to give roundness to the fine squareness of his jaw, and to present him altogether as a very gentlemanly person. And he despised these painters as a clear-headed man could not help despising them ; he detested sitting to them. One of them, Northcote, remarked that seemingly he was accustomed to sit for his portrait.

" Yes," he said very dryly, " my dog Maida and I have sat frequently : so often that Maida took such a dislike to painters that whenever he saw a man take out a pencil and paper and look at him, he set up a howl and ran off to the Eildon Hill. His unfortunate master, however well he can howl, was never able to run much. . . . Yes, I have frequently sat for my picture."

Few people who were introduced to Scott " the famous poet " looked on his face without disappointment. At first sight even to Morritt, who became his lifelong friend and admirer, his features appeared commonplace and heavy, but they continually lit up with varying thoughts. The shy quick glance at his neighbour before bursting into laughter at some good story, the sudden illumination of face, the winning deference that he put on to old and young when he was unfamiliar but was anxious to please, the beautiful vivacity of mouth and eyes—where among his painters is any indication of them ? To one artist, Chantrey, the world is indebted for a character sketch of clear vision, revealing the radiance of his

face. Lockhart is rather deficient in descriptions of Scott's
appearance or habits or familiar thoughts at any period of his
life. The few striking descriptions that exist appear in casual
letters and as illustrations of anecdotes. Yet this man's
life and personality were much more interesting than the
writings that fascinated Europe in his own day.

Walter Scott had a red healthy face, clean-shaven, irregular
in feature and rather ugly ; not much resembling the face with
delicately bridged nose, Cupid's-bow mouth and arched eyebrows that Raeburn, Lawrence, Wilkie, Grant and the rest
painted. His nose was somewhat straight, but I have a sus-
picion that it was somewhat less than straight. His mouth
was a bit off the straight, a legal mouth. As he put on flesh
after thirty-five his jaw grew heavy and his neck Roman, till
at sixty the ruddy sunburnt head and neck were magnificent.
Exquisitely attractive was the irregular mouth. As he sat
silent at his desk, or in his chair, or listening to conversation,
the upper lip twitched softly : it was not really a twitch but
a soft movement more or less continual. Something of this
kind may often be observed in the expressive mouths of the
good-natured. That soft sympathetic mouth of his was always
responding to an impression, but it could close like a vice in
determination to endure or to persist. Impressive, too, was
the length of his upper lip, a common characteristic of lawyers.
In Sir Walter it was simply enormous, for the distance between
nose and mouth was as great as that between mouth and chin.

As he walked along the street his head was always a trifle
downcast, as indeed a lame man's must be, and his eyes were
meditative ; he took little notice of passers-by. But about
his mouth there played the faintest, softest smile, not the grin
that pursues a joke heard a moment ago, but the pleasantest
appearance of brooding over some innocent picture, distant and
delightful. This was his chief characteristic as a boy and a
man. He took pride in recording that the resources of his
mind made his imaginations bright and his spirit happy, and
we have the evidence of this in a thousand details.

He limped, and the limp grew worse when middle age
brought him heaviness and ill-health. In youth a stout stick
was necessary when he walked, and a shoulder was a con-

venience, but after forty-five he had difficulty in getting on even with a shoulder and a stick. Lameness, however, was not allowed to interfere with his development, for as he grew up he combined the bookishness natural to a lame boy with a passion for exercise and the things of the open air. It is pleasant to realise that to the bright spirit of Walter Scott a defective limb was not the curse it was to Byron and is to many sensitive spirits, but was a real source of joy. The sneers and spitefulness of quarrelsome schoolboys, the practical jokes that without a shadow of doubt were devised to torment him, left no impression of bitterness on him. His brooding, happy mind was occupied by the lameness of two ancestors and private heroes of his own, Boltfoot and John the Lamiter. These men had been praised for being lamiters, because they were fighters, active, even famous in their sphere. They announced their lameness, made it a subject of conversation, and enjoyed it. Walter also looked forward to distinction, and if Boltfoot and John had no care about their lameness, neither had he. Before he got a horse he had to depend on his stick, but at seventeen he and his stick had walked so far that Will Clerk, as we have observed, was shocked at the disreputable glaze of his corduroys.

It was about this age of seventeen that his first clear development began. A second blossoming definitely associates itself with his twenty-fourth year or so. At seventeen he wrote from Kelso to his mother that he had shared in rum-grog at a picnic. Apparently she heard the news without concern, and night after night from about that time onwards for seven or eight years he went out to taverns where hard drinking was the rule. It was an age of clubs for real conversation and for hard drinking, and Walter belonged to several. Drinking was the fashion : women had the fashion of being so delicate that they went into hysterics or fainted at a touch of excitement, and men had the fashion of drinking beer, wines and spirits all together for hours on end and rolling about floors and streets, sitting up all night boozing, and heartily despising those who did not or could not carouse with them.

The best description of Scott is that by an old maid, Miss Seward, who saw him first when he was thirty-five. Nobody else has mentioned his striking combination of brown hair, brown eyelashes and flaxen eyebrows.   She thought him rather robust than slender, so at thirty-five he was putting on flesh, though at thirty he had still been of a slim and boyish physique.

We have his own authority, though in a jocular way, for the statement that he had the largest pair of hands in Scotland. His chest was broad and deep, but not exceptionally so.   Hogg, who was smaller, had nearly as much girth as he, but Scott's forearms and upper arms were muscular and tremendous.   It is common for lame people to develop iron strength in their arms.

About his clothes as about his handwriting there were no " curly-wurlies," a word he often applied to decoration in architecture and writing.   He hated to be unshaved, detested " bedgown and slipper tricks " and dressed himself for the day as soon as he rose.

The laird of Abbotsford in the country wore an oldish green jacket, gaiters, and a small blue bonnet, a toorie, from which his hair escaped in every direction.   When he had neither a gun nor a fishing-rod in his hand he had an axe, for he liked to be taken for a mere sportsman or forester, and it gave him embarrassment to be considered bookish.   Till he was forty-five he was as often and as long on horseback as afoot, and liked to be ten hours a day in the open air.

The Clerk of Session in Edinburgh wore a full suit of black, arranged his hair carefully and kept it so, wore shoes with silver buckles, and when at home sat in a highbacked ebony chair in a comfortable study.   He took hardly any exercise, never walked to work though he always walked home, wrought like fury in his study, but remained placid in spite of his intensity and endurance, and took his relaxation at the dinner-table.

His handwriting was a good running hand ; not perhaps quite so fast as the scribble of to-day, but without an atom of special grace or care about it.   There are none of the exquisite curves in it that are quite common in the handwriting of men with some artistic perception ; if he had ever been capable of them they had all been eliminated by strict attention to business.   In his maturity, when writing at Abbotsford in the midst of his family, he was often heard to mutter in disgust, " There goes the old shop again ! "   This was his one large

5

flourish of the pen which in spite of himself he continued to draw at the bottom of his pages, as he had drawn it thousands of times at the desk in his father's office, when finishing off the folios of legal instruments.

When greeting his friends he was accustomed to hold out both his hands to them. He was on familiar terms with all his workmen, doted on his dogs, and even took to his heart the little things he habitually used. Everything that formed part of his personal life was dear to him; at the sale of furniture when he gave up 39 Castle Street, the thought of forsaking for ever some little prints that had once been dear to his wife and that she herself was leaving behind without care gave him wounds of regret.

He had very little ear; no voice; in music he never got beyond a Scotch or Irish song. He had hardly any perception of smell, and when everybody's nostrils were offended he was not conscious of the cause. He sincerely preferred a tumbler of whisky-toddy to the most precious wine ever bottled. He detested cards, though apparently he endured learning the fashionable games. In his generation cards were still a constant occupation of the leisured, but he was not often found at the card-table, that resource of those whose spirits are barren.

He was convinced that he was lazy and idle in grain, but he was capable of enormous industry. When he was apprenticed to his father he vexed that father by his irregular ways of working (" I doubt ye'll never be anything better than a gangrel scrapegut ") and astonished the clerks by his power of application. He once copied 120 folio pages without rest or food. At this time and for some years afterwards he spelt badly, a strange defect in him.

The commonest phrase in old Walter's mouth was " *hoc age*," and it fitted his precise nature well, but it was the last motto in the world for his son. If he had to do anything he had to cajole himself by setting about something else, and then by a kind of perversity common enough he was quite glad to think about the real task. The father thought his son would never do as much good as he might, because he lacked method and concentration. Yet the industry of Sir Walter must have surpassed his father's industry many times over.

Even as a boy he was one of those surprising people who can begin a book at the middle or the end. His fine memory, however, excused and justified his lack of method.

All small irritations that ruffle the tempers of men left him serene, all except the mishandling of books. This was his only spiritual tribute to literature. He disliked lending his volumes indiscriminately, but as one might expect he took pleasure in lending them to those who handled, read and returned them promptly and unmarked.

Among the attorneys who distributed business he acquired no reputation. As an advocate he was a complete failure. This may be accounted for partly by his lack of voice. At the literary or drinking societies that he frequented in his youth he was not a distinguished speaker, and even at the height of his fame he was not eloquent. As he was anything but nervous, and as he had command of language, it is strange that he did not cut a better figure on the platform, but none of his biographers has given us any information to explain this incapacity for public speaking.

At twenty-three the young advocate was arrested and charged before the Sheriff with breach of the peace. There had been a first-class fight with sticks at an Edinburgh theatre on the everlasting argument of Ireland, and Scott had been in the van of an attack on Irish students who refused to sing *God save the King*. He was bound over. At twenty-four he hankered after a skull and cross-bones, and succeeded in obtaining them. This was long before Byron's taste for the gruesome made joylessness fashionable. These pathetic, depressing remnants of a human being like himself were set up as ornaments in his house, and were to be seen in his dressing-room at Abbotsford.

He shaved himself, and his wife was accustomed to cut his hair. Apparently he wore it rather long, so that snippings at the ears and neck were sufficient.

His health required him to take a great deal of exercise. If he went without exercise he suffered from nervous headaches, and his tremendous persistence at the desk was bound to aggravate them, especially when he wrote or read into the small hours. At Ashestiel he changed his youthful habit of sitting up late, began and till he was fifty or more continued to rise at five in the morning, lit his own fire, shaved and dressed, took five minutes at the stable to feed his favourite horse, and was sitting at his desk by six. When the breakfast bell went about half-past nine, he had three and a half hours of undisturbed work behind him. After breakfast he could have a couple of hours more at his desk, and by noon he was his own man. He was accustomed to be out and on horseback by one o'clock, and if any special excursion was on he was ready at ten. On wet days he wrought all day, and he was always particularly inclined to settle down to a good day's work when it snowed.

He had also a rule that letters should be answered on the day they were delivered. With the number of letters he received this was often a day's labour in itself.

" No man ought to be in bed at seven o'clock in summer-time," he said, and bettered his instruction by a couple of hours. At seventeen Will Clerk and he agreed to grind law together. The arrangement was that Walter should to go Will's house one morning, and that Will should come to Walter's next, and so on till the examinations were happily past ; but Will failed lamentably in the matter of rising (though he got through his exams.) and Walter had to tramp to Will's house and rouse him every morning. He was accustomed to go out shooting, coursing, fishing, riding, walking or planting for the best part of every good day at Ashestiel and Abbotsford. Consequently he was often soaked to the skin, and remained for hours in his soaked clothes, laying the seeds of the terrible rheumatisms that he reaped in his fifties. But if he did not mind how often he got soaked he was no practiser of the cold bath. At one time he was subject to sore throat, and believed that he had found a cure in sponging throat, breast and shoulders every morning. After he got rid of the throat he kept up the cold sponge.

He had little use for bridges, but loved to plunge his horse into the fords, even though a bridge were in sight. He was a careless rider and driver. He took his wife in a carriage by steep unmade roads that were not roads at all, that made him wonder at his own foolishness when at fifty he looked at the slopes he had driven down. After forty he grew very awkward at mounting a horse, though he continued for a while as good at a gallop as the next, but after fifty-five he gave up his hunter and reduced himself to a pony. At forty-one his youthful enthusiasm for sport began to leave him, and he confessed that he did not hunt and fish with the relish he had had ten years previously, and that planting and gardening at Abbotsford were much more to his taste.

Whenever he rose from the table his children followed him, and a crowd of dogs barked with joy round about. He had indeed with dogs the way of the initiated, and invariably talked to his favourites as if they understood him. On his first day's journey into the far Borders, after ballads, the house Shortreed and he dined at was that of a farmer, Willie Elliot of Millburnholm. The Border farmer was nervous at the news that an Edinburgh advocate, representative of the law that was the traditional enemy of Borderers, had come to his house. He peeped out of a stable door or from the house window, saw young Walter playing with the six dogs who ran to investigate him, and was perfectly reassured. This man who was so hearty with dogs was a man he could talk to and understand. " Never ten yards," said Shortreed, his guide and companion, " but we were either laughing or roaring and singing." On this excursion Shortreed and he were often drunk, and Shortreed remarked long afterwards that Scott " looked excessively heavy and stupid when he was fou." All his life his good-humour was unfailing ; excitement was almost unknown to him, and even with alcohol he grew not excited but lethargic, and more good-humoured than usual.

He was a great eater. His father was abstemious and his mother lived to eighty-one, so it is not possible to say that he inherited this characteristic from either, but his great mental and physical energy, his violent exercises, and his constant hospitality rendered great eating and a good deal of drinking a necessity. Lockhart, shortly after becoming acquainted with him, seeing him dive into brown bread and kippered salmon, was strongly reminded of the Gilsland lunch of Dandie Dinmont, " who was busy discussing huge slices of cold boiled beef. A large tankard of ale flanked his plate of victuals."

There is a habit among authors of all sorts of mentioning the meat and drink and leaving out the bread, vegetables and puddings. " Huge slices of cold boiled beef," however, leave little room for much else, and there is an irresistible inclination to visualise Scott as eating kippered salmon as another man would eat kippered herring—several.

The cramps in Scott's stomach are thoroughly explained by his lifelong habit of heavy breakfasting. Breakfast was his chief meal. Lockhart said that no foxhunter ever stuffed himself for a day's hard riding with more solid food. He did lusty execution on porridge and " the usually plentiful delic-acies of a Scotch breakfast," whatever they may be, and on a round of beef, or a pie, or a cold sheep's-head. The huge brown loaf stood at his elbow, and the game was " cut and come again."

Every morning a hired cab, called " the Clerk's coach," or " the good ship *Lively*," because it dragged itself so much, went round the houses of the Clerks of Session and carried them to Court. As often as not it appeared at 39 Castle Street before Scott had finished his great breakfast, and out he went with a huge sheaf of bread and meat in his hand and rolled into the ship, with the boisterous laughter of his fellow-clerks welcom-ing him and his last morsel. He ate no more till dinner-time, and then he did not eat very much.

Lecturing the fat James Ballantyne, who suffered from overeating, Scott said that if he himself were to eat and drink in Edinburgh as he did in the country, where he took violent and long exercise daily, it would soon finish him : yet he knew he lived too genially in Edinburgh. And his other habits were as greatly contrasted in town and country. " In the vacation I never sit down : in the session time I seldom rise up."

His eating, however, was mostly done at breakfast, and he was indignant when after his first attack of apoplexy this habit of heavy breakfasting was called in question by the doctors. He swore he would not lessen it by a crumb. As he ate lightly at dinner, the difficulty that besets half mankind in the matter of getting up in the morning did not trouble him, and he has recorded that he slept as soundly on the heather as ever he did in bed. Possibly these sound heather-sleeps were in

Liddesdale with Shortreed or Skene when he was in his twenties.

At forty he wrought with the labourers at Abbotsford, planting trees, making walks and coming home dirty to the knees. To himself the work was indescribably interesting and pleasant. Probably no man ever did so much creation— in planning, in actual planting with his own hands, in altering the whole landscape, and yet in positive spadework and fore-manship—in connection with a manor as Scott did in Abbots-ford. He even created its name. " Abbotsford " was evolved before March 1812, and it is significant that the steading which Abbotsford replaced had been called Clarty Hole.

A beautiful phrase combines his intellectual and rural occupations. " While Tom marks out a dyke or a drain as I directed him, my fancy may be running its ain riggs in another world."

One year a small black pig took a fancy to him and fol-lowed him as often as it could get out, even among the grey-hounds and terriers that were constantly among his feet. Another season a hen was as affectionate and as persistent, and at Chiefswood whenever he appeared there were at one time two donkey mares who trotted from their pasture to lay their noses over the paling and, like the workmen, enjoy a pleasant crack with the laird. The dogs accompanied him into his study and sat round him dozing and yawning for dear life during the three or four hours of taskwork. When he gathered up his papers or lifted the lid of his desk, they realised that they were for the woods or the hills, and leapt up to caress him or whine for joy round him. And it was not only with animals that he was at his best out of doors : he abandoned himself to his friends there also. At table or at the fireside he was confined, but out of doors when he had a particularly good story to tell he stopped and dug his stick into the ground, making free play with both his hands to express himself, while the rest gathered round him.

His reading was always casual, a recreation, not a discipline nor an equipment. This is as it ought to be, but it surprised Wordsworth, who gathered from his conversation that he thought much more seriously of sports and society than of poetry and fame. In his maturity he hardly ever read a newspaper or magazine, and seldom read the reviews, though for a while he took in the *Edinburgh* and afterwards was a contributor to the *Quarterly*. When he finished writing a novel or a poem the sight of it nauseated him, no matter how much praise the educated public bestowed on it.

All his life in order to get work done he had to set himself a task of a certain size every day ; otherwise he grew idle, and regretting the waste of his time went to the other extreme, killing himself with labour. It was his habit to lie in bed for half an hour or even an hour after waking, consciously arranging his thoughts and classifying his situations. At this rate he must have done with very little sleep till he was fifty ; but from 1826 onwards he often drowsed at all moments of the day.

From 1817 till 1819 he had intermittent attacks of cramp in the stomach, now said to be the accompaniment of gall-stones. A terrific and prolonged outburst of those cramps in 1819, when he was forty-seven, definitely broke his health, in spite of various doctors with varying cures. The first definite attack occurred on 5th March 1817, when, at the end of a happy dinner-party at 39 Castle Street, he left the room with a scream of agony. His doctors reduced him to three glasses of wine a day, and the restriction made him sorrowful. At that time he was inclined to blame constipation for his troubles.

When the fiercer cramps began in the spring of 1819 his hair had a sprinkling of grey. In summer, having added jaundice to his sufferings, he was a snow-haired old man. He endured fearful pain, and thereafter his health rapidly worsened. The king's visit in 1822 and the constant excitements that were his daily fare put him into a state almost of fever ; a painful rash broke out on his body and lasted for several years. Thereafter he acquired a long list of ailments— rheumatism, chilblains on hands and feet, gravel, trouble with retention of urine—and every one of them increased his lameness. After he rose from his bed of cramps and jaundice he crawled out on Sybil Grey, yellow, lantern-jawed, decayed in flesh, stooping over the pony's ears, and unable to go above a footpace.

Some of those fits of cramp lasted with the utmost anguish from eight to ten hours, and the only intermittence from pain was fierce sickness. They recurred every third day or so for some months. One morning after a night of terrible suffering he discovered that his legs were drawn into knots and holes, showing that he had had violent cramp in them too, but so intense had been the pain of his stomach cramps that he had been utterly unconscious of the trifle in his legs.

At fifty he felt that he had definitely got two marks of old age : he grew fond of a cat, an animal that in general he had always hated, and he grew fonder of gardening, which he had always despised.

At fifty-four he had a long walk through a plantation at Drumlanrig, apparently with a stick, but without any shoulder to lean on. He fell in with the ladies of the party, but their donkeys outwalked him, and he was reduced to despair when a flock of sheep overtook him and passed him too.

At fifty-five he who had once made a point of answering every letter the day it was received sometimes let letters lie for days unopened.

At fifty-six he records one very depressing day. Thick throbbing at his heart, and fancies thronging in overpowering fashion : an inclination to sleep, and, when he waked, to brood over horrible things. He had been to a public dinner the day before, but it never occurred to him to connect these items. On the following day, 25th October 1827, he received the melancholy letter about Greenmantle from Lady Jane Stuart, and definitely and seriously wrote in his diary that the letter, which was on its way to him but which he had neither seen nor imagined, was the cause of his depressions.

This aspect of Scott was a very real one. He had great interest in murders and would travel far to look around the places where foul murders had been committed : he had a serious belief in premonitions, apparitions, second-sight and the whole apparatus that has taken slightly different aspects in our own day, but is essentially the same now as it was then.

In the winter of 1826–7 his body was very miserable, but in the summer of 1827 he grew better and enjoyed himself a good deal. He loved sunlight, but ill-health made the bright south room at Abbotsford a trial to him, and on 14th July 1827 he suddenly realised that he had been baked and uncomfortable in it for the past two years, and removed his desk to the large library.

When he began to fight against the debts of James Ballantyne & Co. he grudged every minute that he spent elsewhere than at his task. In his diary he detailed time and again the hours and half-hours that his visitors sat before dinner and after dinner. He was incapable of dismissing any one who had any claim to the name of friend ; he had nobody but Anne to help him to entertain them, and Anne was as little interested in them as they were in her.

Most pathetic was his occasional despair. " It is written that nothing shall flourish under my shadow : the Ballantynes, Terry, Nelson, Weber, all came to distress."

There were times when he wrought cruelly at his labours. When finishing *Napoleon* and when he had the whole day to himself, as he had about thrice a week, he started at his desk at 6 a.m. with a clerk, and worked there till 6 p.m. He rose to eat breakfast and lunch, and immediately sat down at his desk again.

In his last years, when very lame and very slow, he had seats placed at intervals between Abbotsford and Chiefswood, where the Lockharts stayed in summer. He took a rest on each as he walked, and carried a book in his pocket in order to read while he rested. In 1830, 1831 and 1832 he had great pain when walking, and hardly walked at all. Even pony-riding became a burden. He had to be lifted on his pony by two men, and the forester Swanston walked at his bridle all the way lest he should fall off. Swanston indeed fulfilled Tom Purdie's duties after Tom died, but to Sir Walter nobody on earth could take the place of Tom. It is hardly a fancy to say that Tom Purdie was dearer to Scott than any other friend. Certainly the Sheriff was dearer to Purdie than anybody else on earth.

His habits of eating and drinking freely rendered the cure or even the stay of his apoplexies impossible. In 1831 after several paralytic strokes, bleedings, purgings, depressions, heart-throbs and a hundred other ailments he still took after dinner half a tumbler or three-quarters a tumbler of whisky and water, or gin and water, apparently with the consent of his physicians. Breakfast remained his chief meal in old age as in youth, but at sixty he described it as " with eggs or in the singular number at least." But what did " with " signify ? Porridge and toast at least, but how much else ? One egg was a matter of laughter to Dandie once on a time. It may be recalled that Bismarck lamented his old age because he could only eat three eggs at a meal. He had once been able to consume eleven or thirteen with joy and subsequent comfort.

In those last years Scott dined at 4 p.m. on soup or broth and a bit of plain meat, probably with bread or potatoes—there is no mention of other vegetables, possibly because he did not consider them worth mentioning : he took no liquor stronger than small beer during dinner, but finished up with the half-tumbler of whisky and water or gin and water ! I understand that beer and whisky together are now recognised as ruination, and certainly I have seen men drunk on one measure of each, taken at the same time between meals. But Scott dined in this fashion every day after his apoplexies began, and he finished up every day with a supper of porridge, which is about the very worst food for any nervous person. When in London in September and October 1831, before setting out in search of health, he saw a good deal of Mrs. Hughes of Uffington, who among other things described his appetite, apparently in wonder that with so good an appetite he did not get well :

" Words cannot describe the fearful change which had taken place since our last meeting. Heavy and helpless, he seemed hardly able to drag his limbs along : a sort of imbecility at times overspread his countenance ; a fixed look of sorrow hung upon his brow : alas ! he was quite sensible of the alteration . . . With me he was always kind and gentle, but I remarked that often to his daughters and his servants he had a fierce impatience so wholly different from his nature that it struck me more than any other alteration.

" He did not dine out anywhere, but kindly said he would make the effort of breakfasting with us. . . . He was cheerful during the breakfast and ate heartily, being particularly pleased with some Yarmouth bloaters."

The day he left Portsmouth for his voyage in the *Barham* he had a " voluminous " breakfast and " dined enormously " on board : he is his own witness and these are his very words. At Malta he was regaled with porter and champagne at dinner —paralysis notwithstanding. Surely all these things argued either great ignorance in the medical profession, or an unwonted lack of restraint in himself.

CHAPTER VIII

THE PERSONALITY OF SIR WALTER (*continued*)

It is not as an intellectual nor as an artistic force that Sir Walter appeals to this generation.   As a poet he never thought much of himself, though the readers of his time esteemed him perfection ;   as a novelist he marvelled at the adulation and the profits that his books obtained.   There is indeed no more in his verse than in Byron's or Southey's ;   it is not the real thing. As a novelist he is outshone by two men now living, or by more.

It is as the exemplar of abounding life that we cherish him. No literary man and few others ever lived a life so rich, so joyous and eager, so successful, so satisfying in peaceful achievements desired and attained.   He was of a nature that everybody loved ;   we have seen that even the stupidest of animals, hens and pigs, followed him about.   Till he was forty-seven he had marvellous health, marvellous spirits.   He associated with everybody ;   he had six months' holiday in the year. Failing in his profession, a nomination to one sinecure after another made for him what to an ordinary man would have been fortune.

And yet his misfortunes are the most rejoicing reading of all.   In them his life riots and revels.   We follow his losing battles with a thousand times the interest we have in his humdrum successes.   In youth there was his passionate first love, ending in rejection ;   he steeled his strong heart and remained himself.   In maturity the crash of his businesses and the subsequent long-drawn-out fight to pay debts that were not mainly his, and for which the law gave him the option of being responsible, is one of the gamest gladiatorial realities on record.   He went into it with incredible passion.   Why did he not avoid it ? Thousands of the respectable since his day have come out of the bankruptcy courts without a stain on their characters, but Sir Walter would not enter them ; he died first.

Few men were capable of enduring prosperity so well as he ; none ever enjoyed better the battle with evil fortune. His aim in life, like his wife's, was to be joyous. He planned his career, his day, his friendships, his occupations, his marriage, with this end in view. He took pride in declaring himself superior to the craving for smoke and alcohol, enjoying the renunciation of them when he felt that he ought to forgo the enjoyment of them. His conversation was chiefly humorous, with strange dashes of incongruous mystery and of brutality, in the roughest details of which he took great interest. It was a boozy age, and its taste was for the horrors. He was rather inclined to be bilious, and he boisterously repressed all symptoms of that unsociable tyranny till the terrific explosion of 1819 mastered him. Then the fire went out of his eye ; then the poor right limb began to drag and grow useless, and his gaiety decayed too.

Hogg, who was the source and cause of more merriment than he ever knew, is the foil against which shines most clearly the fine light of Scott's eternal joyousness. Hogg was convinced that Scott was the author of the famous novels, and John Ballantyne with winks, hints, persuasion and lies had taken great pains to rid Hogg's mind of such a ridiculous imagination. So Hogg was thereafter convinced that Scott had nothing to do with the novels.

Picture then Scott and Hogg going for a walk round the Calton Hill, and Hogg discoursing on the defects of the Waverley Novels. He met a better critic than himself, and a more knowing one. Scott pointed out more real defects in the books than Hogg could ; he heartily admitted all the criticisms as perfectly well deserved, and added others by the dozen.

Hogg was more than ever convinced that Scott had nothing to do with these novels, and every now and then, on pretence of giving his leg a rest, the Sheriff would sit down and laugh heartily at the ridiculous novels.

When he entertained friends with whom he was at ease it was not long before he was excited by his own jocularity ; and when he felt like making fun he could not sit still. Grasping his stick he rose and limped up and down the room, shouting out grotesque things and laughing a loud accompaniment to his speech. His friend Morritt, who was in many respects like himself, became most excited with merriment at table, and always was at his best with wine. As sure as he got to the middle of a story he too jumped up to dramatise the characters of the situation, danced about the floor, and invariably tramped on a dog or upset something. No wonder that Charlotte, who could hardly follow the jokes when they were in broad Scotch, liked the drawing-room.

He was a great lover of the theatre. When he began to make money, one of the first of the miscellaneous hospitalities that were afterwards to make Abbotsford so well known was that extended to actors. He enjoyed their company. The only man who ever made him drink heavily in his middle life was Kemble, who frequently went to Ashestiel. John Macbeth, the fat butler, complained bitterly of the late hours that Kemble brought with him. Kemble, with an obvious pleasantry, met the looks of the butler, summoned at 2 a.m. to bring another bottle, with a flourish of his hand and the friendly greeting of " Cousin Macbeth." The butler of course took it for impudence.

Sir Walter was very fond of spicing his conversation with the devil. One of his most beloved masterpieces of quotation was :

"When the Devil was sick the Devil a monk would be ;
    When the Devil was well the devil a monk was he."

He quoted also the honest old Presbyterian who thought it right to speak with respect even of the devil himself, since no one knew in what corner he might one day want a friend. Apparently the honest old Presbyterian thought that in the next world he might want a cooler corner than he deserved. This joke smells of episcopacy.

" Like the man that met the devil," he says in another place, " I had nothing to say to him if he had nothing to say to me."

But in a generation of swearers—I have seen a reverend gentleman shake his head over the Duke of Wellington as " a bad man : he respected not the name of God "—in a generation of swearers Scott's delicacy was proof against the habit. I have traced, however, four occasions in his lifetime on which he swore, and I bring them out as curiosities, not as blemishes on a great man's reputation. Once he cursed some improvers of the city of Edinburgh ; once, after 1830, he cursed all the political parties of France together ; he swore at everybody the first day the family removed to Abbotsford—but that was to restore order ;—and once, very quietly and gently in his old age, he wrote in his diary, after sitting through some hours of a January day (against his will) while a sculptor mangled a bust of him, " Bloody cold work."

It troubled him to write with his pen if anybody else had used it, and he was always a trifle irritated when he discovered that it had been used. Partly as a measure of careful hospitality, but partly in a vain effort to induce relatives and guests to leave his pen alone, he put blotting-paper, pens and ink into every bedroom and on several tables in the library.

He was not long Sheriff of Ettrick Forest before everything the young Sheriff did, said or believed in was law to the whole countryside. At Ashestiel—it was rather a dilapidated house in his time and it was rat-ridden—he was seven miles from market and from kirk, and about the time of his removal thither he had definitely made up his mind to adhere to episcopacy. His investigations in regard to the Covenanters had convinced him that they were beastly, and " only resembled men in walking on their hind legs " : his influential friends were all episcopalian, and the memory of his father's particular presbyterianism was pungent and abhorrent to him.

Picture then the Sunday morning at Ashestiel, a year or so after the Sheriff took up residence there. For the forenoon the parlour was turned into a chapel, and half the farmers in the district with their wives regularly attended to hear the Sheriff read a sermon and the " English printed prayers." Presbyterians born and bred, they had been taught to believe that people who read prayers out of a book would burn for it, but when they learned that the Sheriff read prayers they refused to believe that it could be wrong, and they trooped in happily to share the homely service.

One of Sir Walter's tastes was partly baronial and partly

great convenience. When on holiday with his family he
ook his own carriage and horses with him.

With the true delight of a wayfarer—possibly his wife,
ike other wives, would not be bothered with such things and
vas accustomed to repose on her husband—he studied his
nap every morning. As often as not he was down the bank
f a stream or exploring an old road, while the carriage pursued
ts leisurely way and awaited him at some point on the highway.

Twice he wanted to be a war correspondent in a generation
hat had more horror of war than ours, and could not even
nagine the trade of describing it. The first time was in 1810,
hen he longed to " take a peep at Wellington and his merry
ien in Portugal," but Charlotte put down her foot and refused
ermission. The second time was in 1815 after Waterloo had
een fought, and Mrs. Scott had no qualms. " I never found
soldier who could give me an idea of a battle," says Scott, who
ched to study the great battle-ground and the fight.

On this occasion he got permission to go, and had the time
his life. He was introduced to all those whom, quoting
adshill in *The First Part of King Henry Fourth*, he called " the
eat oneyers and burgomasters " assembled in Paris, and was
ade as much of by everybody as Wellington and Blücher
emselves.

He had a deep sense of duty that was fostered by his good
ture, and in him took the place of the ideals that less cere-
onious people cherish. He gravely answered as many as he
uld of the letters that unknown correspondents wrote him.
e was on good terms with the most angular people. Charles
irkpatrick Sharpe, who was the sourest of antiquarians,
ned himself to Scott " your devoted slave," and on one
casion, really distressed by the recital of Sir Walter's
ladies, wrote :

" Are you sure, kind, respected, and most beloved friend
my soul, that you keep your feet warm enough ? "

is from Sir Mungo Malagrowther was a tribute of affection
paralleled. But it is curious that Sir Walter himself, in
te of a depth of kindness that has hardly ever been matched
mankind, in spite of extreme endurance of pain and grief

6

on his own part, in spite of his natural courtesy, utterly fails
when he tries to speak sympathy.   He gets literary immedi
ately, loses himself in frightful phrases, and is heartily glad
to shake it all off as soon as possible.   Time and again he ex
presses his own consciousness of being a bad comforter, and
solaces himself with the reflection that it is possibly becaus
he himself is capable of enduring so much.

His nature was not passionate, and it is difficult to trac
any absorbing affection in his life.   I except his first love, fo
his passion for her absorbed him for a few years of youth
But for wife and children he had a strong affection that fitte
into the other details of the day.   For his mother he had
serene love, and his many friends were dear to him in plac
and social ways.

It is easy to picture him in his good-humoured, lazy sin
cerity.   At fifty-five he was as drowsily inclined as at fifteer
when he slept in church.

" One person talking for a long time, whether in pulpit o
at the bar or anywhere else, unless the interest be great an
the eloquence of the highest character, always sets me to slee
I impudently lean my head on my hand in the Court and tak
my nap without shame."

The Clerks of Session sit in a kind of enclosure gazing a
the public : possibly Sir Walter sat immediately under th
judges, and so could indulge in a nap without fear of inte
ruption, but it would have been little of the tricks of a Lor
of Session of those days to have shouted to Colin MacKenz
or Buchanan to oblige him by giving the distinguished auth
of *Waverley* a dunt in the ribs to waken him.   Some of th
judges themselves slept, and this witness has beheld th
judges of later days yawn unendingly.   And Sir Walter w
not always asleep ; he wrote many of his brightest lette
while the advocates pounded the bar—and sealed them wi
wafers because a lighted taper was not allowed in Cou
There were no envelopes in those days.

When his first apoplexy came, his physicians endeavour
to persuade him that it was merely a disorder of the stomac
He was anxious enough to believe them, but found it difficu

" It looked woundy like the palsy. *Well, be it what it may, I can stand it.*"

This was the only kind of boasting he ever indulged in. He rejoiced in the strength that was in his body and soul to resist all manner of evil. It has been said of him that he had no conception of God, and it is partly true ; but no man ever had so little need of moral or spiritual support. In his own soul were infinite peace, infinite endurance, all the resources wherewith man has met the primeval and twilight terrors of life.

He lived in prosperity, but he was a born fighter. He was a true son of the Borderers whose hands were against every man's and against whom every man's hand was. To be outlaws, liable to death at a moment's notice, gave those old Borderers a better conceit of themselves and more strength to their hands ; to be doomed to a joyless old age of drudgery and paralysis (for he realised it only too well before long) steeled his heart for a stronger battle of endurance than any that his ancestors fought.

The details of his helplessness and end may be found by any who have pleasure in looking for them, but they shall not be repeated by me. Enough has been said to exhibit the natural shadows cast by that joyful temperament, that hearty friendliness, that success and achievement ; for the picture of Scott that I like to contemplate is a picture of life as it ought to be lived, with abundant daily joy in tasks, in meditation, in out-of-door pleasures, in reading and study, in food and drink, in family, friends and fields.

CHAPTER IX

THE CHILDREN

THE first child of Walter and Charlotte Scott was born on 14th October 1798, and died the next day.

Charlotte Sophia, who was the eldest child that survived and who was commonly called Sophia, was born about one year afterwards, on 24th October 1799. Walter, " the laird of Gilnockie," was born on 28th October 1801, Anne on 2nd February 1803, and Charles on 24th December 1805. There were no summer birthdays among them. When the fourth child was born Mrs. Scott was either twenty-nine or thirty, and her husband was thirty-four.

Sir Walter, who got on with children after they could mount ponies and understand stories, had no habit of describing their ways, and his letters, full though they are of very many things, are almost entirely silent on the subject of his children's child-likeness, habits and conversation. Often he mentions the spoil of young Walter's game-bag, but though he often repeated the clever things the children said, and clearly they were worth reporting at times, the record of their bright sayings is lost. It has to be confessed indeed that to us Scott's children are rather colourless, and the only reason is that they have had no biography.

Sir Walter lived much with his boys and girls. Though all his life he was full of lamentation about the lack of concentration in the studies of his own boyhood, he took his children from school to the country whenever he went thither, at least until Walter outgrew his own teaching and that of the family tutor ; and as his seat in the Court of Session was vacant for six months of the year there must have been a great deal of interruption in their schooling, and a great deal of trouble to papa, as they called him.

Whenever they wanted to speak to him they entered his study, and were never unwelcome. It was very unlikely that they could have been unwelcome, since the study was free even to the dogs. To sit up to supper was the reward of good bairns; but I cannot quite place supper at Abbotsford, where dinner was always late. Supper, however, they had— probably dessert.

The household was not spared the troubles of children, for in December 1811 the whole four had measles, but happily only a mild attack. It is pleasanter to record that as soon as they could ride they got ponies, were encouraged to make pets of them, to take delight in crossing fords, and to think nothing of tumbles. After small ponies and donkeys were over, when Sophia was nineteen and Anne fifteen, Sir Walter gave them a beautiful pony, a bright bay with a black tail to the ground. They called her Queen Mab.

Papa hated the notion of boarding-schools, and got his girls a governess, Miss Miller, who stayed with them till they were grown, and thereafter was always in and out of a situation and often dunned Sophia for a place among her London friends. The boys went to the High School in Edinburgh, but in the country he himself had to be tutor for the school months the two boys lost. This, however, could not endure, so when they settled at Abbotsford he got a tutor who looked after some of the lessons of Sophia and Anne as well as all those of Walter and Charles. The dislocating yawns with which papa and Walter used to go through the Latin prose were over, and George Thomson, the wooden-legged giant who had qualified for the Kirk but was too eccentric to get one, even with Sir Walter's earnest attempts to place him, tramped from Melrose till Abbotsford grew big enough to spare him a bedroom. He was an original, and everybody said that Dominie Sampson was partly drawn from George. Behold him tutoring the four hopefuls and, after setting them a task, growing more and more absent-minded, more and more wrapt up in a mathematical problem, with his eyes and brain focused to a figure. Master Walter winks to Miss Sophia, and Anne's eyebrows jump to her hair, while fists are shaken at baby Charles who is sure to make a noise. One after another slinks out at the door or window, and it is a full joyful hour till the dominie wakes up and goes in chase.

Sophia

She was called Charlotte after her mother, and Sophia after one of the Dumergue ladies who were Mrs. Scott's best and dearest friends. She was educated at home, and seldom stayed alone at the houses of friends, though daily visits, and long visits with her parents, were common. Twice while she was a girl Sir Walter took her to London and left her with the Dumergues, while his wife and he visited their many friends. Sophia grew up grave and housewifely. In 1819 when Scott had his worst year of cramp in the stomach he was left for a while under her charge while his wife went back to Edinburgh to look after Charles, who was ill too, and to hunt for a cook. Sophia was then less than twenty. At the age of eleven she was in the library when James Ballantyne with natural curiosity asked her how she liked *The Lady of the Lake*, just published. " Oh, I haven't read it," she replied. " Papa says there's nothing so bad for young people as reading bad poetry." And this was no joke. Scott exerted himself to hinder his children from reading his own poetry or any other of the same kind, lest they should acquire any romantic notions of love or life.

The Duke of Buccleuch made a special pet of her and called her his little Jacobite, probably because of the songs she sang, for she was the singer of the family and sang Scotch songs to her own accompaniment on the harp. Curiously enough her singing master was an Irishman, Terence Magrath, who for a while lived in Edinburgh ; but if he endeavoured to cultivate in her a taste for Irish rather than Scotch songs he failed, because of the heartful fashion in which her father rejoiced in the simple Scottish airs and words.

Sophia's engagement to Lockhart was almost as disappointing in its lack of passionate affection as was Walter's to Miss Jobson. On the day of her engagement she wrote to her former governess saying that she wanted Miss Miller to be first to hear the news. And then :

"*I have at last made up my mind* to marry Mr. Lock-hart. . . . That I might have made a much higher marriage in point of rank and wealth I have little doubt. . . ."

" Lockhart " she called him in the same letter.   He himself tells us nothing of his courtship of Sophia, who was twenty and a half when they were married on 29th April 1820.   The whole world that reads knows at least some part of the story of their eldest child John Hugh, or Hugh Littlejohn as he was called.   Precocious, affectionate, ailing, with a tuberculous spine, and doomed to an early death, he found as much a playmate in his grandfather as any of the former generation had found, but of all their intercourse Scott has left no record at all.   He did indeed write *The Tales of a Grandfather* for the boy, but that was chiefly an adventure with the publishers. Sir Walter had found his own boy Charles a great divert and a very precocious child.   When little Johnnie Hugh began to talk, all his speech and all his ways reminded his mother of Charles when he was a baby.

The birth of Hugh Littlejohn was followed on the last day of January 1824 by the birth of a daughter who died two days afterwards.   At the birth of this child Sophia was very unwell and was threatened with the cramps which are common before childbirth and to which her family were probably more than usually subject.   Sir Walter took her from Edinburgh to Abbotsford with a face, as he said afterwards, the size of a sixpenny bit.   Soon it was comparable to a shilling, and with the help of " the black doctor and the red nurse "—the pony and the cow—it soon became a coin worth looking at, half-a-crown.

Sophia's health was seldom good.   At twenty-five she was frequently ill with an inflammation for which rest and bleeding were the treatment prescribed by the doctors.   When she was thirty her father had discovered that she was "a most established coddler " both of herself and of anybody else who was ill, but particularly of herself.   At thirty-two she took rheumatic fever, and on 17th May 1837 at the age of thirty-seven she died, leaving two children, a boy Walter Scott Lockhart and a girl Charlotte.

WALTER

Walter was born in the midst of the flitting from South Castle Street to North Castle Street. " His pipe, being of the shrillest," said his worried father in a letter written that day, " is heard amid the storm of painters and workmen, like a boatswain's whistle in a gale of wind." He was the only one of the four children that Mrs. Scott suckled, and Sir Walter ascribed to this circumstance the fact that Walter was decidedly her pet ; but something must be allowed for the fact that he was her first boy. He hated books and loved to be out of doors. His father found him remarkably gentle and sweet-tempered, but like all healthy boys he was wild, and no doubt as quarrelsome as other schoolboys.

In 1810, when he was nine and at the High School of Edinburgh, he came home one day with blood and tears staining his cheek. It was just after the publication of *The Lady of the Lake*.

" Well, Wat," said papa, " what have you been fighting about to-day ? "

Walter grudgingly admitted that he had been called a lassie.

" Terrible ! " said Mrs. Scott, " a terrible thing ! A frightful insult to be called a girl ! "

" Ye may say what ye like, mamma," said Wat, " but I dinna think there's a waufer thing in the warld than to be a lassie, and sit borin' at a clout."

Wauf is waif, shabby. Boring at a cloth was Walter's notion of sewing. But let those who are on the look-out for a new joke repeat with all the emphasis they can Wat's denunciation of lassies, especially lingering over " borin'," and they have made a discovery. " Waufer " is a word that has almost perished, but any other suitable word may be substituted.

" How did you happen to be called a lassie ? " asked papa, pausing in his soup and wondering that such a name should be applied to wild Wat.

" Snippety Clever and me was arguin', and, says he, ' Lady *of* the Lake ! Lady *of* the Lake ! ' Was I going to take that frae him ? "

" And what do you think he meant by calling you Lady of the Lake ? " asked Walter Scott, with emotion in his voice and in his heart.

" I don't know.   How should I know ?   Lady is the same as lassie, isn't it ? " . . . .

In the first year of Abbotsford Walter was still a small boy, and when he discovered Cauldshiels loch he bought a toy boat to sail on it.   At least once it stuck in reeds or weeds, and the Sheriff had to take off shoes and stockings and wade in after it.

His talents did not drive him to read or write verse, though his tastes and his father's were very much alike.   His own particular hero was Johnnie Armstrong the freebooter, laird of Gilnockie.   He harped so much on Johnnie that the " uncles " —the other Clerks of Session, who were frequent visitors— dubbed him " laird of Gilnockie," and after a little while as " laird " he became once and for all " Gilnockie."

As Walter grew up his sisters discovered that he was rather vain when he got into new clothes.   When he joined the Yeomanry at seventeen they lost no opportunity of pointing out how proud he was of his Yeomanry uniform.

" Papa asked him lately what his brilliant genius " (a real sisterly touch) " inclined him to, and he declared that he would be nothing but a soldier."   When he got into the uniform of a cornet of Hussars his sisters prophesied that he would die of conceit before ever he saw his regiment.   Even when he had a wife of his own to tease him his sisters could not leave him alone. In December 1826 he had hopes of being sent a-soldiering to Spain or Portugal, and as he rampaged up and down declaring what his men would give the Dagos, Anne with a vacant stare was singing loudly :

> " Oh set me on a foreign land
>   With my good sword intil my hand
>   And the king's command to fight or die,
>   And show me the man that will daunton me."

" Gilnockie, my man," said one of Sir Walter's colleagues to him when he was about nine or ten, " ye canna help seein' that great folk make mair work about your father than about me or any of your other uncles—now why is this, do ye think ? "

The boy pondered a little and answered gravely, " It's commonly him that sees the hare sitting."

He joined with great joy in the sports of his elders. He was keen on gun and rod, on greyhound and horse. Indeed his horsemanship was considerable. He could do everything with a horse that a man could do, and while yet a lad he trained his pony to perform all the feats that might be seen at Anstey's. At fourteen he was a bold horseman, a fine shot, and otherwise so earnest and helpful that his father called him his gamekeeper and took pride in taking him on all errands out of doors. At a football match at Carterhaugh in 1815 the men of Yarrow met the men of Selkirk at a game of 100 a side. Before the match began young Walter carried the banner of the Duke of Buccleuch round the haugh, and as he was well mounted and newly dressed in green, with a green cap and an eagle's feather in it, he was a great swell, and attracted much attention by his bright horsemanship and boyish dignity.

In July 1819, when he was less than eighteen, he joined the 18th Hussars. By this time he was six feet one and very strong. His outfit, purchased in London with the experienced and expensive John Ballantyne to advise, was in Sir Walter's opinion abominably extravagant. It cost £360, and a couple of horses cost another £200. Thereafter his allowance was fixed at £200 a year. His first station was Cork, and when he arrived the colonel wrote home to Abbotsford laying down the law in some matters. Walter was only to have two horses, was not to change them without the colonel's consent, and on no account was to keep a gig. Sir Walter heartily agreed with all items, especially the last. " You know of old," he wrote to his boy, " how heartily I detest that mania of driving wheelbarrows up and down, when a man has a handsome horse and can ride him." He proceeded to give Wat a great deal of wisdom about the kind of horse not to buy and the kind of acquaintance not to buy from—the kind that sells a spavined or broken-winded animal as a favour.

Sir Walter missed Wat for many reasons, but wrote that he missed him particularly in the matter of getting the rest of the family up in the morning. No doubt Sir Walter, who was not only punctual for breakfast but who usually had three hours' work behind him when he came hungry to his mighty meal, fretted when Lady Scott, Anne and Charles came straggling in to breakfast. Apparently it had been a standing job of Wat's to hound them out of bed every morning.

It was when Walter was about twenty-one that he first met Miss Jobson, the fatherless niece of Sir Adam Fergusson, Sir Walter's neighbour and lifelong friend. The little lady was proprietress of Lochore and was very well off. To the worldliness of the arrangement by which these two people were matched and married let Sir Walter himself speak. He wrote to his son on 9th March 1824 in these terms :

" Something has happened last week which I can only hint to you in a mystical kind of way. You must know Sir Adam and Lady Fergusson brought their niece Miss Jobson here to dinner, who seems a very sweet, pleasant young woman and has none of the conceit of an heiress about her. Now Sir Adam made a sort of explanation to me of his and his lady's views towards the young lady, to understand the nature of which I beg you to read over the first scene of *The Merry Wives of Windsor*, supposing yourself Mr. Abraham Slender, that I am representing the worshipful Justice Shallow, and our friend Sir Adam Sir Hugh Evans, and that a lady already named is sweet Mistress Anne Page. I understand she is to pass the summer or part of it at Gattonside House, and if you have courage to make the attempt you will have plenty of opportunity and, as Sir Adam thinks, a fair chance of success. I need not point out the great advantages on the lady's side, but there are some on ours also which would make the match not so remarkable, though there were as many wooing at her as at Tibbie Fowler of the Glen, renowned in song.

" Now if you think this matter worth prosecuting it will be necessary that you be at Abbotsford in the summer. . . . I have only to add that Sir Hugh Evans is of opinion that Mr. Slender will not be crossed by the influence of any Mr. Fenton.

" If you desire to break off the matter entirely you will let me know immediately."

Then in a P.S. : " ' Five hundred pounds and possibilities are good gifts,' says Sir Hugh Evans."

The lady was worth a great deal more than the five hundred pounds of the quotation, and young Walter came post-haste from Ireland to secure her. He was then six feet two and uniformed in imposing style, and Miss Jobson was on the small and slender side : she was impressed by the whiskered cavalry-man and accepted him. Never was a more mercantile marriage arranged.

But witness Justice Shallow's surprise—the surprise of the romantic poet—when the plan went all right and the money was secure. On 23rd January 1825, nine months after the plan of campaign had been drawn up, he wrote to Mrs. Hughes :

" My son is just about to be married : the young lady is a very considerable heiress. . . . Truth is, there had been some little kindness between the young folks about two years ago, and though they had not met again till lately, yet hearing much of each other through Lady Fergusson, the wife of my old friend Sir Adam, they had neither of them, it seems, forgotten their intercourse, but had in our Scottish phrase *thought on*, till our Christmas gambols brought out little Cupid with his linstock and fired the mine."

To Miss Edgeworth he wrote :

" Cupid mingled with our Christmas gambols, *and we learned with some surprise* one fine morning that the lady had agreed to carry the young hussar's knapsack."

I cannot resist quoting Wordsworth, another and a more sublime poet, on the subject of marriage and money. His nephew wanted to marry the poet's daughter, and Wordsworth sat down and wrote this reply :

" If you have thoughts of marrying, do look out for some lady with a sufficient fortune for both of you. What I say to you now I would recommend to every naval officer and clergyman who is without prospect of professional advancement. Ladies of some fortune are as easily won as those without, and for the most part as deserving. Check the first liking for those who have nothing."

No wonder Scott, who prided himself on his gentility, called Wordsworth " every inch a gentleman." They were remarkably alike.

There was a great ball at Abbotsford at Christmas 1824 in honour of the engagement. This was the first ball given at Abbotsford, and in Sir Walter's time the last. The couple whose courtship was so romantic were married on 3rd February

1825. To this lieutenant of twenty-four his father thereafter, if not before, addressed his letters, "Walter Scott, Esq., etc. etc." In the same year Sir Walter bought him a captaincy and paid £3500 for it. He became lieutenant-colonel and retired with that rank. The romantic marriage was a fruitless one, and the baronetcy died with the second Sir Walter.

He never settled down as laird of Abbotsford, but chose to go to India with his regiment about 1839. In August 1846 he took fever, which culminated in liver disease. He sailed from India in the *Wellesley* and died on board, near the Cape of Good Hope, on 8th February 1847, at the age of forty-six.

CHARLES

When Charles was a small boy of six his father was convinced—like so many more parents—that this sharp lad would make a name for himself. " The little fellow, if it please God to spare him, will turn out something uncommon, for he has a manner of thinking and expressing himself altogether original." This pathetic prophecy, often repeated, gave way at length to the conclusion that Charles would be clever enough if he cared, but that he did not often care. And it is specially unfortunate that not one of his smart sayings as a small boy is recorded.

At eleven his father described him as " excellent at play and not deficient at learning, when the young dog will take pains." When he was twelve Sir Walter turned Washington Irving over to him with the information that Charles was quite capable of showing and describing Melrose Abbey. At fourteen he rode to one of the fairs in the neighbourhood and made himself sick with sweetstuffs.

Sir Walter had a horror of laziness and idleness. He blamed himself very unfairly for both, and discovered the same qualities in both of his boys. To Charles he wrote : " Your great deficiency is want of steadiness and of resolute application to the dry as well as the interesting parts of your learning." Indeed Charles as a lad was such a scatterbrain that his father contemplated sending him to India, the dumping-ground for the lazy and incorrigible of that generation. He hoped, however, that Charles would settle down to study, and had fixed on the diplomatic service as the sphere in which his great influence would be of most advantage to his son. Accordingly, when he was almost fifteen Charles was sent to a tutor at Lampeter in Wales, and Sir Walter had to complain of the sixteen-year-old Charles as of all the rest of the family : he could hardly be persuaded to write. After a long course with the tutor Charles passed to Brasenose, where at twenty-two he took his B.A. At twenty-three, by the interest of the king, he was appointed to the Foreign Office, and while in London he stayed with the Lockharts. After some time in the Foreign Office he was sent to the Court of Naples. It was unfortunate for him that Lockhart's biting pen offended the Whigs, who had a long spell of office. His juniors were openly promoted over him, and it was well understood by everybody that the reason was not incapacity on the part of Charles, but the mere fact that the editor of *The Quarterly* was his brother-in-law.

He had a slight deafness even as a boy, but the degree of deafness depended on his health and spirits. His father thought it a nervous affection, and was sometimes troubled because it made the boy abstracted and absent-minded.

In 1825, through Mrs. Hughes of Uffington, he was introduced to the Duke of Buckingham, spent some days at Stowe and wrote home to his sisters about it. " How he got there Heaven knows," wrote Sophia the sisterly, who had not then heard of the introduction. " His letter was full of what the Duke said to him *and what he said to the Duke.*"

As he matured his health was indifferent : he was very miserable for long periods with severe inflammation of the eyes and with rheumatism. The warm climate of Naples, where he remained for a few years, banished the rheumatism, but it returned with him to England. In 1841 he went as an official with a delegation to the Court of Persia. He took fever and died at Teheran, where they buried him : he was only thirty-five.

ANNE

Anne was the excitable member of the family, and though Charles was the latest I fancy that Anne was the baby. All the children learnt French at their mother's knee, and it is recorded that Anne at least forgot it utterly.

She was subject to fainting fits, but so were all the women of that generation. Possibly this was due to some national defect in dress or diet, but if so I have not come across the explanation. It could hardly have been all sham, for fainting is not easy. The day that young Walter left for the Army, a proud Cornet of Hussars, Anne went into hysterics over him. When driving in a closed carriage to and from balls and parties during the years when the Radicals were giving concern to the Tories, Sophia lay back on her cushions and accepted the dangers of closed carriages at their true value, but Anne peered out continually, saw a Radical in every man they passed, and instead of the brooding visions of youth before and after dances she had premonitions of broken windows and women torn out by the hair.

She was very frank and bright in conversation, with a habit of insinuation and innuendo which was rather obscure but was startling when discovered. Like the rest of Sir Walter's children she was without any kind of pretence or affectation.

Of her looks, as of Sophia's, there is significant silence on the part of everybody, and it is certain from their portraits that they were very plain. She was quick in talk and hasty : her letters were never finished without postscripts, clear evidence of impatience. When trouble came, Anne's way of bearing it was recorded by her father. " She is stout-hearted and courageous in important matters, though irritable in trifles, . . . bears her misfortune gallantly and well."

In 1831, when she was about twenty-six, she had an offer of marriage, and to her former governess she only mentioned it after the man had married another lady with a great deal of money, which, Anne had since found, would be very necessary. " After mature deliberation I rejected my little ——" she wrote.

To Anne fell the terrible task of nursing first her mother

through the fearful asthma and final dropsy, and then her father through all the irritations and strain of his apoplexies. Sophia was married and away to London, and though Thomas's daughter Anne, cousin of the Lady Anne, was a tower of strength to the household, yet the two Annes had a twelve-hour day apiece, besides the times when they were both required. I imagine that Sir Walter made an ungovernable invalid : his great bulk, his mental strength and an obstinacy unparalleled must have made the lot of his nurses a terrible one.

These burdens killed Anne. In February 1831 Sir Walter wrote in his diary that she was very nervous, but it can hardly have occurred to him that her race was not long to outlast his own.

At Christmas 1832, three months after the death of her father, Anne obtained a pension of £200 a year from the privy purse of King William. But her constitution had been shattered in the course of her long and painful attendance on her father and mother, and Lockhart hints at personal disappointments consequent on Sir Walter's diminished fortune. From the day of his death she was never well, and she died at Lockhart's house on 25th June 1833, nine months after her father, at the age of thirty.

With great possessions and means of enjoyment this family was singularly unfortunate. Sir Walter died at sixty-one, having lived the last eight of these in ill-health, disappointment and continuous over-exertion. His wife died before she was fifty, and the record of the children is appalling. Sophia, the eldest, had her heart wrung during most of her married life by the illness of her eldest child John. She herself was often ailing, and she died at thirty-seven. Walter, the baronet, died at forty-six, childless. Charles, troubled all his life with deafness, sore eyes and a good deal of rheumatism, died of fever at Teheran when he was thirty-five ; and Anne, the baby, the espiègle, the audacious, had all the accumulated misfortunes of the house loosened on her poor head, was worn out in terrible conflicts with ill-health and misery, and died at thirty.

It is amazing what humankind can come through. Sir Walter's mother lived to see eleven of her thirteen children dead ; yet the day before she finally took ill she was as jocular and happy as she had ever been.   Anne was of a different fibre, and indeed probably so were the other three.   Joyful and free childhood they had, but much they had to afflict them in their short lives.

CHAPTER X

FAMILY LIFE AT ABBOTSFORD

I. The Building of the House

ON 28th May 1812 the Sheriff flitted from Ashestiel to Abbots-ford. All his peasant neighbours turned out to enjoy the pro-cession, about the only kind of spectacle that in the secluded valley of Tweed they ever witnessed. Old swords, bows, targets, lances, old muskets and banners were conspicuous in the procession ; a new-hatched brood of turkeys was lodged inside an old iron helmet ; the cows and the sheep, the horses and carts, the pigs, the poultry, calves, ponies, greyhounds and spaniels were led by a dozen ragged boys, who carried fishing-rods and spears. There were " twenty-four cart-loads of the veriest trash in nature," said Sir Walter himself.

When the procession reached Abbotsford, six miles down Tweed, everything went wrong. The horses refused to go into the strange stables ; the cows and sheep ran out of the pasture as soon as they were put in ; the hens flew out of the yard ; the kitchen fire would not burn ; the oven would not bake ; the jack would not go ; the pump would give no water : the men swore, the maids wept and Lady Scott scolded. Everybody in turn came into the little room in which Scott had taken refuge and complained about the rest. At last the Sheriff was unable to endure it any longer : he went out in a tremendous rage, swore a bit, and in half an hour everything and everybody were in their right places.

The masons began immediately to enlarge and rearrange the existing cottage, Clarty Hole. The novels had not then been begun, and Sir Walter's notions of Abbotsford were to develop greatly with the stimulus of the profits from printing and publishing the Waverley series. Meantime there was nothing but discomfort. All that year he had no room to himself. The only parlour that had been made habitable served for drawing-room, dining-room, schoolroom and study. A window looking to Tweed held his desk ; an old bed-curtain was rigged up to separate him from the uproar of the rest of the room, and within that enclosure he wrote *Rokeby* and much else. The women gossiping, the children squabbling and playing or repeating their lessons, made no impression on his iron nerves. He had all the long months of summer before him : besides the easy labour of writing he had his real enjoyment and taskwork of planting. He was not going to lose a moment in setting out the oaks and larches that were to adorn Abbotsford in the future ; he began planting immediately ; he did spadework with ditchers, foresters and drainers, and also attempted some of the tasks of the building workmen. In all the bustle Tom Purdie was the happiest and most important man in the world, except Scott himself.

His first purchase in the matter of Abbotsford had been " a small farm, value about £150 yearly," in 1811. When he announced his lairdship to Morritt he declared that he had only fixed two points : one, that the garden was to surround the house ; the other, " that the little drawing-room shall open into a little conservatory, in which conservatory there shall be a fountain. These are articles of taste which I have long determined on."

He considered the situation of Ashestiel much more beautiful than the situation of Abbotsford was when he took it over, but it had none of the woods then that later he gifted it withal. His description of Clarty Hole, which he renamed Abbotsford, was " a bare haugh and a bleak bank by the side of the Tweed, on which I design to break a lance with Mother Nature and make a paradise in spite of her. I have the Tweed for my henchman for about a mile : I should not otherwise speak so crously." He said too, though partly in joke, that all his friends had abused him for buying the ugliest place on Tweed.

With supreme passion and violent haste Sir Walter set about his tourney with Dame Nature : with superficial carelessness he described his battle as " wearying themselves "— he included his wife, whom at first he dragged all round the little estate—" all day in looking at the improvements they had in hand." In January 1813 he had fixed up a nursery for forest trees, had got larches from Loch Katrine, was busy banking and dyking against the river, and planting willows, aspens and weeping birches round the new old well. Without scruple he collected carved stones from the ruins of Melrose Abbey near by and used them in the masonry he set up to cover the same well. By the first spring too he had planted a fine background of copse with large trees in front, an instalment of the future landscape of Abbotsford. In March seventy acres had been planted.

The house, " a little scrub place," had been occupied by people called Redford, who apparently had farmed the place themselves. It is to be remembered that the farms of Ashestiel and Abbotsford were actually carried on by Sir Walter. He was the farmer, and he disliked the job, could not acquire much enthusiasm for a good crop of turnips or oats, or even for a prosperous spring of lambs. To him the planting and cultivation of trees were the most delightful occupations of Abbotsford, and he changed the face of Nature in the square miles he owned. Day after day, year after year, he rambled and wrought in the fields and on the braes; he sowed in his own nurseries; he planted trees with his own hands; thinned them with his own axe and saw; and at length saw the crow building in them.

To James Pringle, Scott was crawing crousely about the trees he had planted at Abbotsford. " It will be long till the crows build in them," said Pringle, to damp him; but on an April day in 1826 Sir Walter, with sensations of supreme joy, utterly thwarted by the fact that the estate was in the hands of trustees, watched a pair of houdie-craws building in one of his young oaks.

The summer of 1813 was exceptionally warm, beautiful and serene, and Sir Walter was worried to death with trouble in business, for already he had to meet bills that he had drawn against the firm, to renew them and to pay them. The long list of those bills never seemed to cease, and he could not get John Ballantyne, who was cashier of the printing firm, to warn him what to expect.

By that time the children had a garden of their own, which had been nicely kept, and the main garden too had been brought into order. Many friends had contributed ; among them the Duke of Buccleuch's head gardener had sent him some fine fruit trees.

In December 1814 young Walter alarmed everybody by taking smallpox. He had been vaccinated as a child, and was vaccinated again when he took the disease. A day's shooting of wild duck at Cauldshiels, with much else, had to be postponed, and the family were greatly relieved when the illness was over without infection of any of the other children.

Pets were multitudinous in those early days when the children were young. In 1813 the family donkey died, and Scott had to soothe Lady Anne with a peacock and peahen, both of which were very tame; but he laid up trouble for himself, because the peacock declined to roost with his hen in the place allotted to him and found a place under Sir Walter's window where he spent his nights, keeping the Sheriff awake with screeching and lamentation. Another pet was a large raven called Ralph who had a remarkable power of speech, far beyond that of parrots. It died of a gorge of food, and Scott used to lecture James Ballantyne, who was given to overeating, on the sad end of poor Ralph the Raven.

The turkey cock and his forty or fifty hens were scarcely pets, but they had the run of the grounds, and Sir Walter complained to Charlotte that they ate up all his shrubs. With a touch of the grotesque that always tickled Sir Walter she met his remonstrances with the demonstration that after all it was really himself who was eating the shrubs, since in good time he was to eat the turkeys.

If the children had their pets Sir Walter had his little games which he elevated into idolatries and which gave Wordsworth the impression that he was little more than a trifler. At an early date the museum at Abbotsford was an institution, and was discussed by the whole family. Scott wrote to Sophia the great news that he had got a lock of Charles 1.'s hair for it. Even to-day visitors to Abbotsford may behold unbeautiful small wisps labelled the hair of this and that celebrity.

From the very first years of Abbotsford he was pestered to

death by visitors. In September 1813, in the midst of the racket of building, congestion in the house, planting, writing and business vexations that worried him, he complained that his temper was worn to the breadth of a hair. An " intruder " hung on him from one day till twelve the next day, and just when he had taken up his pen two other loungers arrived, as pat as the relief of a sentry.

About 2 a.m. on two nights of April 1818, while Abbotsford was still abuilding and the house was exposed, there were mysterious noises in the part that was unfinished. The second time the noises occurred Charlotte was really frightened, and Sir Walter got up with Beardie's broadsword under his arm but found nothing and nobody. He was certain it was " these idle fellows called workmen," who were skylarking about the buildings. In the daytime his own two girls spent most of their leisure on top of the scaffolding. Sophia declared that it would be a wonder if the house was finished without one of them breaking her neck.

When the dining-room was completed in 1818 they had John of Skye in every evening with the bagpipes, and to that frightful music they danced nightly.

The building of Abbotsford is roughly divided into two periods. The first plan of the house was worked out by 1818, but in 1821 Sir Walter obtained plans for the completion of the house and it was finished in 1825. Not much short of a dozen amateur and professional architects have left their mark on Abbotsford. Scott himself designed several details, including the gateway and the screen between court and garden ; the masons of Darnick did the work. Terry was his principal adviser all through, and Skene also was much consulted. The professional architects who supplied plans that were definitely used included Mr. Blore, Mr. Atkinson, Mr. Bullock and Mr. Stark.

II. Friends and Guests

It was from deep and long experience that Sir Walter called a house a devouring monster. From his earliest days of housekeeping he had always kept open house for friends. At

Ashestiel the number of constant visitors increased, and at Abbotsford the thing became almost preposterous. Every one who came to the neighbourhood with any social pretensions or with any introductions expected to be asked to stay, and whether they came from Fife or France it was all the same. At Ashestiel the house was full when ten people got into it, but it sometimes held thirty. At Abbotsford while bedroom accommodation was still scanty the guests sometimes climbed ladders and slept in lofts over the stables or over Peterhouse. There was a continual scramble of guests from 1812 till 1826, the year of the crash and of Lady Scott's death. Thereafter the visitors who were received were comparatively few.

But though peers and princes, travellers and celebrities, passed nights or weeks at Abbotsford all the year round, the intimate family life succeeded in surviving. Sir Walter was a typical British father of the prosperous type. He had no interest in his children as infants. On the whole he got peace and leisure at home from the noise of and labour over infants, and he took his children about with him when they grew big enough to mount ponies or to trudge. He sent Charles away from home at fourteen, because it was clear that if he stayed at home he would never study, and he took great pains to arrange suitable marriages for Walter and Sophia. The girls were fonder of carrying their secrets to him than to their mother. In the everlasting crush and incoming of visitors the family intimacy grew and kept its own character, and a circle of constant friends kept steady place among all the crossings and interruptions of strangers and acquaintances.

The number of Sir Walter's friends whom he received along with the casual important and with each other was as large as it was varied. First and foremost was Sir Adam Fergusson, and not only he but all the Fergussons are too interesting and mixed too much with the Scotts to leave undescribed. Adam Fergusson, the kind of jolly bachelor who marries at fifty, a singer, a joker, a social success, was Sir Walter's lifelong friend. In 1917 Sir Walter bought the lands of Toftfield for £10,000. The house of Toftfield he rented to Fergusson and changed its name to Huntly Burn. From 1817 till 1821 Adam lived with his sisters at Huntly Burn, on the estate of Abbotsford, and during these years the two families were constantly together. Scott continually referred to Sir Adam's sisters as " the cailleachs "—the very old women. Sir Adam's favourite songs were " Johnnie Cope " and " The Laird of Cockpen "—this after Mozart, Schubert, Handel and the other song-makers had lived and died. Indeed all the songs they sang at Abbotsford were rather pathetic ; it is death to the musical to go on with the same stuff for ever. Sir Adam was a bachelor till 1821, and Sir Walter attended the baptism of his own first grandchild and the marriage of this schoolfellow in the same week. In spite of knocking about in the Army, and though loudly humorous in company, Sir Adam was modest, shy and even a trifle diffident. When angling for an invitation from Cadell the publisher who had given Sir Walter a day's outing and " tiled whiting " at Cockenzie, his gentle manœuvres were exquisite to behold, though he might have said " Take me next time." One of his standing jokes, which hit off Sir Walter's extreme views both in politics and in tune, was to sing " Awa', Whigs, awa' " with great gesticulation and in a horrible cacophony. It was the pleasantest part of Sir Adam's character that though he was a first-class wit when he tried, he was screamingly funny whether he tried or not. In 1818, when he got his title and his job as Keeper of the Regalia of Scotland, he took over about eleven acres of land, and thereafter went round all the farmers, ploughmen, carters, foresters, ditchers, drainers, shepherds and tradesmen in and about Darnick, telling them all about it and asking their advice about the way he ought to work his farm.

His youngest sister Margaret was very like him in humour and in ways of thinking. She was exceedingly wrapt up in Sophia, who for her part found her in 1835 "not very sane."

The eldest, Miss Bell, was very much of an old maid, grave and shy, but kind, motherly and without any sourness. The second, Mary, was very pretty in girlhood, but she became deformed and grew peaked and thin. She was accustomed to rise very early in the morning, and roamed a great deal over the wild land about Abbotsford and the Eildons, wearing on her head the most complicated pile of handkerchiefs of different colours. She was apparently considered quite mad by the neighbours, whatever may have been her real condition.

Other lairds in the neighbourhood were Pringle of Torwoodlee and Scott of Gala. These Scott often met, often dined with, and oftener hunted or fished with. Pringle was a relative of Lockhart's, Scott's future son-in-law, and this may partly account for Sir Walter's keen interest in Lockhart at and immediately after their very first meeting. The other Clerks of Session who sat at the same table as he for six months of the year were all special friends who were often at Abbotsford, and in whose houses in Edinburgh Scott and his family were often to be found. These were all called Uncle by the young Scotts. They were David Hume, a nephew of the historian ; Hector Buchanan, a Highlander ; Sir Robert Dundas ; and Colin Mackenzie, who had been his friend from boyhood.

Ashestiel is only half a dozen miles up Tweed from Abbotsford, and the owner, Colonel Russell, was a far-out cousin who with his two sisters was made welcome at Abbotsford when they came. Pringle of Whitebank was nearly as far away, but was near enough to ride down or to meet the Sheriff on the moors.

Besides the friends who dined and stayed, there were many yeomen and farmers of whom Scott had a high opinion and with whom he and his family associated a good deal. One of these was John Usher, formerly owner (laird) of Toftfield. Usher ultimately farmed the lands he had sold, and was often to be seen with the Sheriff at salmon-fishing or the hunting of hares. Park, a brother of Mungo, was another farmer friend, and the other farmers or small owners of the district were all Sir Walter's men. These people were all familiar with the Scotts, and came and went regularly for twenty years, but there were others who came and departed. Lockhart estimates that in his seven or eight most prosperous years Sir Walter entertained as many distinguished people as any noblemen anywhere ever did. And the most pleasant part of the Abbotsford entertainment was that when a marchioness or two with their lords, a lawyer or two, an old schoolfellow, a far-out cousin, a local dandy or laird, a mamma with daughters, and the family all sat down they were as merry under the bright eyes of the Sheriff as though they had all met again after painful parting.

A German prince was expected to pass Abbotsford in October 1819, and possibly to call. Early one morning while Mrs. Scott was still in bed Sir Walter returned from his study to his bedroom and said he would not be surprised if the German would expect to be asked to Abbotsford. A prince, even a German one, was a prince before 1914, and Scott was startled but not surprised at his wife's reception of the news. " I wish you had heard the scream she gave," he wrote to Walter.

" What have we to offer him ? " asked the mistress of Abbotsford, just as other men's wives ask.

" Wine and cake," said Scott, thinking to make all things easy ; but in utter despair Charlotte looked vacantly about and said :

" Cake ! Where am I to get cake ? "

She sent searchers to prowl through the whole city of Selkirk for cooked meat, and managed to get one shoulder of lamb. It was all housewifely fuss, however, for when the German sat down there were boiled salmon and blackcock and partridge.

Lady Scott accused her husband of the three sins that beset a Scotch landlord—overwalking, overtalking and overfeeding his guests. No doubt it did some of them good to be overwalked and harm to be overfed, but there is no doubt that none of them suffered from the overtalking, a treat without parallel in that generation in Scotland, unless perhaps the sufferer was Sir Walter himself. He seldom sat in any particular seat at his own dining-table, but if he was not carving dropped into the readiest place. This casual way of insisting on comradeship was typical of him. He considered it his duty to talk to his guests, no less than to feed them. He ate lightly at dinner, and so could be jolly without regret. A favourite story of his was that of the goldsmith in Edinburgh who made a fine host, and when asked how he managed to attend so well to his guests replied that he always had a steak and a pint of claret half an hour before the guests appeared.

III. Servants

Sir Walter's servants occupy a place in history that servants have never occupied in the whole course of time. This humane and large-souled man, who was a stickler for rank and position, was in the nobler parts of his nature a true democrat : he was never for one instant so absorbed by his own importance that he did not spare a part of every command, of every phrase, for clear recognition of the personality of the person who was doing his work. The small great are a sealed book to their servants : their emptiness is too clearly recognised by any conversation whatsoever.

When guests came to Abbotsford the chief treat, in Sir Walter's opinion, was not to be introduced to the casual duke or marchioness who was there, but to listen to Tom Purdie. Minor joys were a walk to the bowling-green to hear, on the other side of the hedge, Peter Mathieson and his family singing their evening psalm with the cottage door open, a turn round by the sawmill where the woodcutters were busy, a day's fishing with Charlie Purdie, and the examination of Melrose Abbey under the guidance of Johnnie Bower with his blue coat, red waistcoat and quotations. And if Johnnie was not a servant of Scott, he was a fervent disciple.

We know too little about any of them ; we would like to know a great deal more of them all, especially of Tom Purdie, whose heart swelled within him in the twentieth year as in the first year when the lame laird gripped his collar and was dragged along. We do know that whenever anybody was engaged by Sir Walter he sent a fiery cross round the hamlets of his relations, urging them to come and share the good fortune he had found. This was no small compliment to the Sheriff, and it probably suited his temperament, for he was inclined to the clannish system, in which the chief or the laird has a personal interest in all his dependants and they are all more or less related to each other.

Willie Laidlaw, the factor of Abbotsford, was the son of a farmer, and like so many Borderers and Scotsmen delighted to think himself and be thought " a gentleman." Scott met him first in 1801, when on one of the hunts for ballads he discovered a crowd of originals on the one hillside—Laidlaw, Hogg, Hogg's mother, and Hogg's uncle, who at eighty had turned religious and abominated the ballads and gladness of the days of his strength. Laidlaw was then working on his father's farm, Blackhouse, and was a mere youth : later he himself took a farm, but failed. Providence, which always looks after the sentimental, directed Sir Walter to buy the lands and house of Kaeside in 1817 shortly after Laidlaw went bankrupt, and as Kaeside was empty he offered it rent-free to his friend " till some good thing turn up." To the house he added grass for a cow and other perquisites. At first Willie was probably expected to give some indefinite assistance in return for house and perquisites, but he soon developed into a full-time factor for Abbotsford.

He was a pronounced Whig, but took care not to argue with Sir Walter on politics. His assets were a tall, imposing figure, a modest aptitude for writing, a sentimentality that expressed itself in frequent tearfulness, and a habit of flattery that disguised itself under an air of simplicity. It is difficult, in spite of all the books written about Scott, to get a grip of this man, his chief servant. There is no trace of any emphasis in anything that he ever did, said or thought. Yet when Lockhart was at Chiefswood and the Fergussons were at Huntly Burn none of the parties was considered complete without Laidlaw, so some charm he must have had.

Scott's influence immediately got him a post as writer of a monthly article in *Blackwood's Magazine*. This he resigned very quietly and resignedly a few years after-wards, because he was disgusted by the manufactured ravings with which *Blackwood's* pandered to the appetite for hatred that was then so large a portion of the mind of the Tory party.

His favourite phrase was " What for no ? " of which Sir Walter made good use, and which is the only literary survival of Laidlaw. He was the kind of man who has a lot of daughters and no sons.

Sir Walter took pleasure in having in his employment the best wrestler, the best cudgel-player, runner, jumper and shot in the district.

After Tom Purdie was promoted to librarian-in-chief and personal attendant, the post of head shepherd was given to Robert Hogg, brother of the poet. He was also butcher to the house, killed their mutton and beef, cured their bacon, and probably made puddings black and white, haggises and the rest of the " Scotch dainties."

Hogg the real shepherd was rather ashamed of the fame of his brother the Ettrick or idle Shepherd, realising only too well that it was ruination to the naturally flighty James, who made his house a free hotel for admirers as long as he had any money or credit. One summer the shepherd was very seriously ill and his own whole stock of twenty lambs died. When he recovered Laidlaw took him to task in a way that hardly looks like a joke. " This is very strange, Hogg. I fear you've been to blame in something, for none of Sir Walter's sheep are dead, and yours are all gone." " Aye," said Hogg, "it's like it may be for a punishment, and weel deserved, for when I was as it seemed on my deathbed—God forgive me— I had mair thought and care for the twenty lambs than for the state of my poor soul." It is to be explained that the shepherds of those days had little or no wages. Their interest was tied up with that of their masters, for they were given several sheep, whose wool, lambs and mutton were their per-quisite. If they did not attend to the flock their own animals were as likely to die as those of their masters. To-day, as a hundred years ago, this custom holds on the Borders, though besides some annual lambs a shepherd before 1914 had fifteen shillings a week and a cottage, and seldom left his hillside except to go to the market.

It was James Hogg who brought in his brother, and a nephew (who may have been the Abbotsford shepherd's son) became a printer's reader, a badly paid post requiring great intelligence and accuracy, in the works of James Ballantyne & Co., Edinburgh. Laidlaw tried to settle an old uncle of his, a Cameronian minister, as chaplain and tutor, but the proposal came to nothing. Tom Purdie, as we have seen, brought along his brother-in-law Peter Mathieson, who was thence-forth the family coachman. Peter soon learnt Sir Walter's ways, and on passing any landmark or site of importance in Edinburgh or on any roadway Peter unbidden would rein in his horse to something less than a walking pace to give the Sheriff time to gaze, to explain or to expatiate. As often as not, especially on the winter week-end drives from Edinburgh to Abbotsford and back, the Sheriff was on the box talking to Peter.

Scott laid out a bowling-green near Peterhouse, as he called the cottage of Peter. He built an arbour on one side and declared that he meant to have a game of bowls every evening, because that was part of the old *vie de château* that he wanted to resurrect. But he afterwards confessed that he put the bowling-green and arbour there so that he could listen to Peter and his family singing their evening psalm at the same hour each evening. His evening stroll, when there was no game on, was oftenest in that direction, just to listen to the singing of the family.

In 1826, after the crisis, Peter put off his leisure and his standing, and in his old age turned ploughman in Sir Walter's service rather than seek the ornamental position anywhere else—and it may easily be assumed that Sir Walter Scott's coachman, especially in that year of misfortune, would have been eagerly sought after if he had chosen to go. Peter put on rough clothes again with equanimity, and only donned his livery on high occasions. It is possible that his plough was pulled by a yoke of oxen : at any rate ten years previously the pair that ploughed were Og and Bashan, well known to the neighbourhood. As the greater part of the estate was in the hands of trustees Laidlaw had no option ; he had to give up his factorship, and leave Kaeside. He stayed for some time with a relative at a farm about a dozen miles distant, but after four years he was enabled to return.

John Bruce, besides being a hedger and ditcher, was the " Highland piper " at Abbotsford. His pipings are silent, but his cure for Sir Walter's cramps is still as subtle and sweet as the melodies of his most melodious instrument. He spent a whole Sunday wandering over the countryside, and selected twelve stones from twelve south-running streams, so that Sir Walter should sleep on them and be cured. In the midst of torments that would have made any other man dismiss the alchemist with a sound cursing, Sir Walter's playful appreciation of the absurd rose to the occasion just as sweetly as if he had been at ease and in that very mood. The piper got a message that the recipe was infallible, but that it was absolutely necessary to success that the stones should be wrapt up in the petticoat of a widow who had never wished to marry again. John Piper in despair gave up the attempt at cure.

Another hedger on the estate was Davidson, called Captain Davidson because he had led his companions at some fight or other. By the fall of a big stone in November 1821 this " faithful and honest servant " got a leg badly hurt. It was the funeral of his little daughter Anne that Sir Walter was late for, on the occasion of showing Mrs. Hughes round the grounds.

John Winnos was forester under Tom Purdie, and it is possible that though Tom was opinionative in the matter of trees, John was skilled. Both set up to be oracles, and were much consulted by everybody, partly in a teasing way but oftenest in good earnest. John Swanston was partly agricultural labourer, partly forester. At the beginning he had charge of the estate sawmill at Toftfield, but after Tom's death he became henchman and Sunday pony to the laird. John Moodie had similar jobs. Joseph Shillinglaw, the carpenter at Darnick, was often employed at Abbotsford. Like everybody else, even before Sir Walter had avowed the authorship of the novels, Joe took it for granted, and called his terrier Rob Roy. He was the best marksman Sir Walter knew, and he had such a passion for shooting and ran off to shoot on so many occasions that his widowed mother, whose only son he was, worried herself and him lest he should end in neglecting his business. This, however, Joe gave her no good reason for assuming ; he was a good and steady workman, and in order to get shooting he often rose at 3 a.m. to get at hooded crows before work or breakfast. The big table that stands in the library at Abbotsford is entirely Joe's work, and it was made in that room, the Sheriff as wrapt up in the process as Joe.

At Ashestiel the butler was Macbeth, but the butler of the happy years at Abbotsford was Dalgleish. Sir Walter never had what one could call a valet. In 1826 he came to the conclusion that a butler was thenceforward out of the question, so he tried to dismiss Dalgleish, who wept, made a scene, and definitely refused to be sacked. But his health gave way in 1830 ; he had to retire, and John Nicolson succeeded him. John was handsome, warm-hearted, intelligent and serene ; he was good at games, and Sir Walter had applauded and taken pleasure in his skill. Something of the daily devotion and intelligent care that he gave his master during those two terrible years of the oak's decay may be gathered from Lockhart's tribute to him : " His name is never to be mentioned by any of Scott's family without respect and gratitude."

John had been in the household since he was a boy, and was a general favourite. When Scott went abroad in search of health John was instructed how to use the lancet in order to be able to bleed his master, and he performed the operation several times. When in 1827 Sir Walter took a furnished house at 6 Shandwick Place he took John Nicolson with him, and in 1832 Morritt took John as his butler to Rokeby.

Of Mrs. Mackay, the housekeeper at Abbotsford, I have no other information than her name. Celia Street was Anne's maid and was almost as great a help as John. She went from the Scotts to Lockhart's house in London, and in 1836 married a brewer at Walworth.

In the winter of 1816–17 Scott kept about thirty labourers employed in and about Abbotsford, partly to relieve the distress of that year, for unemployment was rife, partly to plant the great stretches of woodland, to fence them in and thin them. He was on intimate terms with many of these workers, certainly with all those who were constantly in his employment. When in 1815 he returned from Waterloo and Paris he took home presents for the workmen, including a snuff-mull for one of the old men. When Sir Walter met him again and asked for a pinch of snuff he was surprised to see the old man draw out his old horn box.

" Hoot, man, not that old mull," said the Sheriff. " Where's the bonnie French one I brought you from Paris ? "

" Troth, your honour, sic a mull as that is not for weekdays."

One of the Abbotsford workmen was old John Fraser, who gave Sir Walter a word that he often used in his diary and in talk : " I was not very *cleever* to-day." Another, a forester, comes down to fame briefly as John the Turk, because of his affection for the other sex.

Another old man, Tom Watson, toddled down from Falshope to see how Sir Walter was getting on when he had the wild cramps. " If anything ailed the Shirra it wad be sair on the Duke," said the old man, and Scott was greatly pleased to hear of the saying.

Though apparently not in Scott's service, Charlie Purdie, brother of Tom, was much in the company of the Abbotsford family. He was accounted the prince of fishermen, and he had charge of salmon-fisheries for three or four miles of Tweed. His cottage was at Boldside, on the north bank of the Tweed, about a mile above Abbotsford.

Though so free and hearty with servants and working men, Sir Walter did not share the usual fate of those who condescend. Something about him, an explanatory, smiling temperament, commanded efficient service; he was indeed a very rigid enforcer of discipline. Few men were so well served as he, indoors and out, so carefully, so respectfully and so silently. But his interest in all his fellow-men had no condescension about it. He talked to every man " as if he was his blood-relation," as one of the workmen said. If the footman was handy in the carriage he talked to him ; he insisted that young John Nicolson should do some lessons daily and bring his copy-books weekly for inspection. When he went avisiting he invariably stopped at door or carriage or on the stair to have a word with those servants of his friends whom he was in the habit of meeting, and knew.

IV. IN THE HOUSE

Abbotsford was the paradise of dogs : every room was open to them. And they formed the subject of some pleasant teasing of the head of the house, who was no more held in outward reverence by his children and familiars than other heads of houses are. A word often in Scott's mouth was the " tail " of a Highland chief, that is, the following of vassals and kinsmen. Lady Scott and the whole family, who could hardly ever get near him for the retinue of dogs that nosed after him and gambolled about him, called the dogs his " tail." Every time he rose from table, went up a stair or went out of doors they clustered about him, leapt to his shoulder or bounded on in front. I never imagine him limping from the door but

8

I see a greyhound doing its wonderful gyrations of joy at his leg and just missing him at every bound. " Dogs and cats all well, and send remembrances," he wrote to C. K. Sharpe, who was an uncanny *double* of himself in mind, tastes, language and pursuits, though as unlike as possible in person.

Lady Scott was as fond of dogs as her husband was. Her beautiful spaniel Finette was a special favourite of everybody, and poor Charlotte was greatly annoyed in the autumn of 1820 when Finette absolutely refused to leave the joys of Abbotsford for Edinburgh and her.

Greyhounds were kept in the house and were continually used for coursing. Not fox-hunting but hunting the hare was the most popular sport at Abbotsford, and the Sheriff enjoyed it best of all, probably because there was more boisterous fun for the whole crowd in it than in fishing or shooting. No presentation of Scott is complete unless it includes his great love of fun and his everlasting laughter. He remembered and loved thousands of stories because they tickled him to death continually. It was great fun to be soaked with rain on the hills, soaked to the skin. When his boat was rotten and plunged him into Tweed, when the carriage rocked and lifted crossing the ford in a high water, when a hotel boots at Moffat wanted to fight him, he roared with joy. Everything that happened to him was enjoyment—till the infernal cramps of his forty-eighth year came.

At least one visitor to Abbotsford found that an air of punctuality and method without any waste or ostentation pervaded everything, but this I do not entirely believe. The good things of Abbotsford followed the family regularly to town and helped to keep down the bills for household food and entertainment. At least once a week while the family was in Edinburgh a huge basket of provisions arrived by the carriage or the carrier or public omnibus—butter, cheese, eggs, vegetables, jars of cream, fowls, game, rabbits, hares, salmon and trout. Sir Walter thought of having mutton and beef also brought to town in winter, but I find no evidence that this was arranged. On days of removal from Abbotsford to town it was the rule that the whole Scott family should dine with the Skenes.

In those days the Court did not meet on Mondays, and so besides the vacations of nearly six months and the New Year fortnight, there were many week-ends to be snatched at Abbotsford in winter. Under his gown when he appeared at the Court of Session on Saturdays he wore not the usual black suit but a green jacket and country clothes. At noon Peter was in Parliament Close with the carriage, and Scott was off in great joy to Tweed. From 1826 till his retirement from the Clerkship of the Court of Session those frequent winter week-ends at Abbotsford were dropped. His work suffered little diminution because of the excursions. His mind worked by flashes of illumination : he thought off and on all day about the story he was working on, and when he came to write it down he never hesitated.

There were two annual festivals at Abbotsford in the years of prosperity. The first was a great day of salmon-fishing for " the gentry," who gathered under Champion Charlie's auspices and, assisted by his precautions and wiles, usually managed to get great baskets. At the end of the day the salmon, boiled, grilled, and roasted, were served up under a great ash tree beside Charlie Purdie's cottage at Boldside.

The second festivity, the joy of tenant-farmers and yeoman neighbours, was the Abbotsford Hunt, usually held on 28th October, young Walter's birthday. The hunting was the hunting of the hare either on the moors above Cauldshiels Loch or over some of the hills of Gala. Between thirty and forty dined at Abbotsford in the evening, and one of them, a farmer, was known to declare to his wife when he arrived home safe that his only desire in the world was to go to sleep for a year less a day, because there was only one day in the year worth living for, and that was the Abbotsford Hunt.

Neither the wooden leg nor the religion of the dominie, George Thomson, prevented him from sharing in the Hunt. He had another innings too when they sat down to dinner, ravenous as they all were. The dominie stood up and said grace a mile long, first praising God for having given man dominion over the beasts, and then giving a religious and thoughtful turn to every incident of the day. Sir Walter would fumble with his spoon, hardly able to endure it. When the dominie sat down, "Well done, Mr. George!" he would say. "I think we've had everything but the hulloo."

The only accident that ever befell the revellers at this series of dinners befell Hogg. Tight as he emerged from Abbotsford, and chaffed for being exceedingly tight, when his pony was brought to him he laid a bet he could leap over her as she stood. He leapt, fell—and Lockhart who disliked him said he broke his nose at the attempt. Possibly he meant that he broke the skin of his nose, but there is no other evidence on the question whether it was broken skin or broken bone.

Sir Walter had been accustomed to spend Christmas with the Duke of Buccleuch at Mertoun House, but the Duke died in the year of the removal to Abbotsford, and thenceforward Scott's festivals were kept at his own house.

At Abbotsford much was made also of such national festivals as Hogmanay. On New Year's Eve 1824, when a large party was assembled to do honour to the completion of the house and the engagement of young Walter and Miss Jobson, they sat up till midnight, but it was a ponderous evening. Long blank pauses occurred and then a feeble whisper, but little more.

He thought it uncanny, that is, a temptation of Providence, not to welcome the New Year in the midst of his family and friends, and with "a het pint." Yet on Hogmanay of 1825 he was so utterly exhausted that he stole away from the waiters on the New Year and went to bed. The New Year's ceremony that gave him most pleasure was the series of visits that he, the laird, received from about a hundred children of the estate on Hogmanay. The children came in groups or families and went away rejoicing in a piece of cake, a bannock of oatcake and a penny.

This patriarchal interest in the children signified more than pleasure in bright faces and the bestowal of gifts. All Sir Walter's relations with the people on his estate and with the public were inspired by a grave sense of his own duty as the possessor of property that others lacked. Nothing on earth, for instance, would induce him to put up boards threatening prosecution to trespassers or poachers, and he loved to see the children nutting, even though they might be damaging his hazels.

But the splendours of Abbotsford and its rising attractions gave anything but joy to one upholder of the importance of another house.

Pringle of Whitebank and Yair had made a fortune in India. Yair House was pleasant to behold, and Thomas the butler of Yair was an old man who beheld with annoyance the building of Abbotsford and the concourse of great names there.   In time the butler retired on his savings and on a pension, but he continued to live at Yair, weeding the garden, showing the house and grounds to visitors, or attending on the ladies of the family. He was never tired of inquiring what parties were at Abbotsford, and the more they were and the more important the sound of their names the more miserable was he.   In summer-time he was always in a fever of jealousy.

He could not find fault with the Sheriff, but he was greatly down on Lady Scott, on all her arrangements and doings, and on the supposed excellence of Abbotsford itself.   He objected to the use of cedar wood for Sir Walter's library and thought oak would have done well enough.   Lady Scott's dress did not please him, and he freely distributed his opinions of it and of her.   He quizzed everybody who had been at Abbotsford about what was happening there, and was only happy when there was something at Yair that he thought superior.

It was highly amusing when the old servant at Yair criticised Lady Scott's doings, but it was serious when Sir Walter's own hunter threw him from mere dislike, and just as serious when Lady Scott's best housewifely efforts met with blank disregard and unconsciousness, though exercised under her husband's nose.

When he returned from his first excursion to France he was eager to see his hunter Daisy, who was brought round to the door to be petted and mounted.   But after so long a separation the horse absolutely refused to be backed by Sir Walter.   Daisy was pure white without a speck, with a great mane, and had always had what was to a lame man the valuable quality of standing like a rock to be mounted, but when Sir Walter caressed him the horse looked round like a devil, and when Sir Walter put foot in the stirrup he reared bolt upright and upset his master once, twice, thrice.   Thereafter the poet, glad enough of the excuse, stuck to cobs, for he was growing heavy and slow, and had little chance of escape if he were severely thrown.

But if Sir Walter was disappointed in Daisy, the whole household was disappointed in him. During his absence Charlotte had introduced new chintz into the tiny drawing-room of the early cottage that was Abbotsford. The new furniture was very bright and attractive ; Mrs. Scott and the girls had been looking forward to enjoying the great pleasure that the little surprise would give the lord and master. He was received in the bright room, sat down comfortably in one of the new chairs, laughed, talked and related his experiences with increasing gusto, while the faces of wife and family lengthened and drooped. He was entirely unconscious of any change in the arrangement of the room. At length Charlotte could no longer contain herself, and drew his attention to the new furniture. Sir Walter was greatly vexed at having caused such a disappointment, and every now and again he threw out a word of admiration of the chintz, for the consolation of mamma.

The boot was on the other foot with a vengeance a few years later. When the whole civilised world was aware that Walter Scott had left Edinburgh and had gone to London in order to be made a baronet, the baronet-elect was complaining to his son-in-law-to-be that though he had been away from wife, daughters and sons for nearly three weeks and had written home many letters, he had not had a scrape of the pen from any one of them. He arrived in London on 15th March 1820, and on the 30th he wrote to Lockhart, who had written in order to solicit Sir Walter's influence in procuring a professorship for Christopher North, "I am very angry with Castle Street. Not a soul has written me except yourself." On 3rd April there was still no letter, and he wrote to Sophia, "The people here are like to smother me with kindness, so why should I be in a great hurry to leave them ? Indeed, I don't see why I should not stay here, as I seem to be forgotten at home."

At Castle Street they were all preparing for Sophia's wedding the following month, but the chief reason for their silence was that letter-writing was bothersome.

Two of the minor plagues of life at Abbotsford were rats

and Major Weir. The rats were always everywhere and Major Weir was never anywhere.

They could not get rid of the rats, though a rat-catcher was employed season after season, year after year : indeed they did not seem even to diminish.   It is said of rat-catchers that they invariably leave some rats undestroyed, lest they should lose their occupation, and in the case of this particular catcher Sir Walter was convinced that he made no effort to destroy the rats but spent his time talking and laughing with the servants. In 1831, immediately after a political meeting that had disappointed him extremely, Sir Walter met the rat-catcher, who suggested that he should come along to Abbotsford and finish off the rats as he had promised to do for nineteen years past. Sir Walter looked at him gravely.   " Go to political meetings," he said, " and you will find plenty of rats there." And he walked off.

For Sir Walter's lameness a heavy stick was a necessity all his life, and especially in middle and old age.   But that walking-stick was uncanny ; it was never to be found. " Where's Major Weir ? "   " He's vanished again."   " I swear I saw it in the hall a moment ago."   " Here it is.   Who put it here ? "   " Nobody."   With such shouts, with laughter and the turning of irritations into joy, the walking-stick, Major Weir, was found.   Major Weir in the flesh had been burnt at Edinburgh in 1670 for being in two places at once and sometimes nowhere at all, and it was the irrepressible Anne who nicknamed the stick.

Besides the Scotts themselves there were two cousins who stayed at Abbotsford, children of Tom Scott, Sir Walter's brother.   In 1821 young cousin Walter came to stay permanently at Abbotsford and Edinburgh, and his sister Anne followed in 1826, as we have seen.   This Anne, like the other, was comely and pleasant, though not beautiful.   Her coming delighted her cousin Anne, and she proved a tower of strength to the harassed family.   For harassed they were.   The six years from 1826 to 1832 were one long misery to all of them. They killed daughter Anne in the flower of her womanhood, and there was no joy in them for any of the others.

The last year of real health and of happiness for Sir Walter was 1824. In that year he lost Sir Adam Fergusson, who was bought out of the house at Gattonside, to which he had removed when he married.

In the summer of 1830, when the burden of debt had grown less and Laidlaw had returned to the cottage at Kaeside, Lockhart with wife and children came back once more to Chiefswood, and Scott, though much broken in health and unable to walk, was happy in their company. He still conformed to the diet prescribed by his doctors, but in the evenings he looked jaded and worn. The chief pleasure he had was to pace Douce Davie through the green lanes of his own woods with the grandchildren clustered about him on ponies and donkeys, while Lockhart, Laidlaw and the women on foot pruned and marked trees as he directed.

CHAPTER XI

TOM PURDIE, THE FRIEND AND TYRANT

In July 1804 the Sheriff of Selkirkshire, pestered by Lord-Lieutenant Napier, who insisted that the Sheriff should no longer be a carpet-bagger from Edinburgh, but should have a house within his own jurisdiction, took a lease of Ashestiel, which is rather " up," as Abbotsford is just a bit " down," Tweed. He was only a little while settled in his new house and farm when a poacher was brought before him on the usual charge. The poacher pleaded guilty in a talkative and humorous way of his own ; he declared that he could not get employment, that he had a wife and a crowd of bairns to provide food for, and that the only way to get food was to take the grouse that were at his doors. He fairly compelled the Sheriff to let him off, possibly on some formality. The poacher got the astonishment of his life when he was offered the job of shepherd on the Sheriff's farm of Ashestiel. He jumped at it, and so Sir Walter Scott got his tyrant, the affectionate, proud, dour and faithful Tom Purdie.

In 1804 Tom was thirty-seven and the Sheriff was thirty-two. In townless Ettrick a farm was almost a necessity for Sir Walter, and as it was not so much a shepherd as a shepherd-manager that he required, Tom soon received full authority. It was also part of his duties to keep watch over the house while the Scotts were in Edinburgh, and if in the dark winter days Tom may have longed for the return of the master, Sir Walter himself has recorded that he " pined for the hillside and the sweet society of Tom Purdie." And again, " I shall be glad to be at Abbotsford, to get rid of the town, where I have not, in the proper and social sense of the word, a single friend whose company pleases me. In the country I have always Tom Purdie."

Exactly twenty years after they met, Scott, writing *Redgauntlet*, drew a picture of Tom, who was then about fifty-seven. " His brow was not much furrowed, and his jet-black hair was only grizzled, not whitened, by the advance of age. All his motions spoke strength unabated, and, though rather undersized, he had very broad shoulders, was square made, thin-flanked, and apparently combined in his frame muscular strength and activity, the last somewhat impaired, perhaps, by years, but the first remaining in full vigour. A hard and harsh countenance, eyes far sunk under projecting eyebrows which were grizzled like his hair, a wide mouth furnished from ear to ear with a range of unimpaired teeth of uncommon whiteness and of a size and breadth which might have become the jaws of an ogre."

Poverty, unemployment, and poaching (which included the risk of mantraps, spring-guns and thrashings) had soured Tom's naturally hard temper, but the air of Ashestiel and Abbotsford was a dissolvent of sourness, and Tom's bitterness became a sort of dour blitheness. He kept up some contempt for those who could not shoot nor fish with credit, and was particularly angry with the biggest salmon he ever saw because it had been caught by an English guest—who turned out to be a Scot with an English accent. Tom was always happiest, and his face shone with delight, when any of the guests at Abbotsford whom he did not like got into trouble. When Constable, very fat and gouty, was following Sir Walter up and down through the rough ground and through the terrible heather, protesting as he sweated and panted that there was no other poet on earth after whom he would dance in such a fashion, Tom was in ecstasy, lingering behind Sir Walter to enjoy the sight of Constable's efforts.

Tom took a measure of the Sheriff that nobody else took. He was the Sheriff's man. His heart swelled when the collar of his coat was grasped by his master, whose increasing weight was accompanied by a more painful limp : his pride was to be with the Sheriff, and he claimed interest in the very novels— " our buiks " he called them. But out of doors he was the elder brother, much more experienced in everything, and the Sheriff was to be instructed. Even when he had to give way to Sir Walter, it was clear that he did so in order not to give offence, and that he continued to believe his own opinion and his own way much better.

For a long time Tom was confined mainly to the shepherd's job, but it is plain that he disliked it. Scott loved to have him when walking, and after the removal to Abbotsford and as the young woods grew the shepherd was gradually transferred to the woodlands. As the Sheriff's lameness increased the sturdy shoulder became a necessity. " What a blessing there is in a man like Tom, whom no familiarity can spoil, whom you may scold and praise and joke with, knowing the quality of the man is unalterable in his love and reverence to his master! Use an ordinary servant in the same way, and he will be your master in a month."

When walking in rough weather Tom carried Scott's plaid, and told long, long stories, dating perhaps twenty years back, about hits and misses with the gun. When the Sheriff developed rheumatism Tom insisted that their walks on cold, windy days must be by the sheltered ways, even though his master pleaded for the exposed braes and hills. They must have looked like a tall and a small brother as they wandered through the woods and the heather. When Lady Scott issued her decision that the Sheriff's clothes were getting shabby, the white hat, the green jacket, and the breeches were given to Tom, and the Sheriff got a new suit, so that Tom must have seemed another Sheriff, more alert, browner, and smaller. The fact [that one was tall and the other short would have given a tailor some concern, but probably it did not worry Tom.

As the woods of Abbotsford grew the Sheriff's joy was to thin them with his forester. Both wore belts, and in the belts of each were an axe, a chisel, a small saw and a hammer. If it was a big task, requiring the help of the labourers, the Sheriff spent the day with them, and all were invited to supper at Tom's cottage. But even during the years of Tom's shepherding his occupation was broken by the claims made on his time for fishing and shooting excursions with Sir Walter, and with numberless guests who had to be entertained while Sir Walter was busy at " our books," for odd jobs about the house, and for many miscellaneous affairs out of doors and in. He was after the Sheriff's own pattern, eager to be abroad, a good shot, a good fisher, a phrase-maker, strong in prejudice and hardy as the heather.

It was an incident in Tom's career as a shepherd that was responsible for Sir Walter's constant references to himself in his journal as S.W.S. The morning after that on which the news of the baronetcy reached Abbotsford, Tom was not to be found in any of his usual haunts, and he remained away all day. The other shepherd and he spent the whole day marking the sheep with an additional letter to signify " Sir," so that the beasts that had been marked W.S. now bore S.W.S. Tom also ordered one of the masons who were busy on Abbotsford to carve the S. on the stones that marked the boundary between Abbotsford and Kippielaw. This item of calling a mason from his work is one indication among many of Tom's authority.

The marking of sheep was very much in the manner of Tom's signpost. For the convenience of guests and strangers he erected in the woods of Abbotsford a signpost, and with his own hand painted on it, " The Rod to Selkirk." This brought him great fame, as Mr. Polly's sign of " Omlets " on the river brought much custom to the little inn.

Until he became pained with walking Sir Walter never rode on Sundays, not from any scruple about the day, but because he considered that a horse was no less entitled than a man to a weekly holiday. His " Sunday pony," as he called him, was Tom, and the Sheriff laid heavily on Tom's coat-collar with his left hand. Tom was as joyful as a proud steed when the Sheriff got him in his grip, and no easy grip it was. It was on a Sunday, and it was with Tom, that the most beautiful recorded incident in Scott's life happened. There was a little dispute between Tom and him about the thinning of a hedge at Huntly Burn. Sir Walter had given some directions or advice that had not been attended to, for Tom was neither to be convinced nor directed. When they moved on it was no longer Tom's collar that Sir Walter had a hold of, but Constable's, and Tom dropped gravely behind.

They approached a gate, and Tom sprang forward to open it.

" Give us a pinch of your snuff, Tom," said the Sheriff

when they had passed through, and his face, which had been vexed, cleared up.

Tom's mull was brought out, and this time when they moved on it was again his Sunday pony that Scott had. When they came to the house, Sir Walter, Constable, and Lockhart sat down on chairs outside, and Tom, who ought to have taken himself off, lounged about. At length he asked the Sheriff to give him a word in private, and the two walked off into the garden. Scott reappeared alone, and his face was one smile of delight.

" Will ye guess what he has been saying now ? Well, this is a great satisfaction. Tom assures me that he has thought the matter over, *and will take my advice* about the thinning of that clump."

An exquisite relationship between master and man ! The man, dour, opinionative, hard-hearted, and utterly unconcerned at disobeying his master when he thought the master was wrong, but appalled at the least estrangement ; the master, an expert, ruffled for a moment at disobedience, but whole-heartedly banishing the whole matter from his mind and resuming his familiar ways in a moment, without any submission on the one hand or rebuke on the other. And Tom's way of putting it !

As the years passed episodes like this must have been plentiful, for Sir Walter has recorded that Tom generally contrived to be master. " Now and then I am restive and insist upon my own way ; then comes the tug-of-war. Tom retreats and reappears in about two or three hours with ' I'm thinkin' whether ye're no richt in this matter, and I'm no sure I'll no tak your way.' "

Evidence abounds that Tom thought much more of his own skill than of the directions his master gave him, the master whose pride it was that he had had the best teachers and had read all the best books on planting. " Tom is very costive about trees," complained Sir Walter to Laidlaw, " and talks of only 300 poplars. I shall send at least double that number. Don't let Tom forget hedgerow trees, which he is very unwilling to remember. He thinks he is saving me money when he is starving my projects, but he is a pearl of honesty and good intention."

Tom had a half-bred pointer which he called Di Vernon when she pleased him. Di became an exceptional favourite with him, and he went about boasting of her cleverness. If he stayed longer than he should have stayed at the public-house and mixed just one more tumbler than he ought, Di was accustomed to jump up, take him by the sleeve, and howl. When shaken off she had more than once fled home and brought Mrs. Purdie, whom, of course, there was no resisting. We know that Abbotsford was the home of marvellous men and dogs, but this story nevertheless exhibits Tom in the guise of a liar, and it is to be hoped that his discourses with the Sheriff were not so barefaced.

When the wild cramps came in 1819 one of the attempts at treatment was a scalding bath. Immediately the cramps came on, Sir Walter was stripped and flung into the bath, and smallish Tom was there with his sinew and strength to heave and hold the great bulk of the Sheriff—" like a haulded saumon," he muttered grimly as he struggled with him. I am sure that in his agonising pain the Sheriff summoned a smile in appreciation of Tom's excited comparison.

Tom was free of the house inside as well as of the woods and hills outside. No matter how ceremonious the occasion, or how many people were present, it was a rule that when Sunday dinner was over Tom came in to drink long life to the laird, the lady and the company, in whisky or wine as his taste varied.

In March 1826 he was definitely released from all shepherding and miscellaneous farm work, and was made forester—a great day for Sir Walter and Abbotsford when the woods definitely had their keeper, and no less of a day for Tom, who loved the woods, and loved better the company of the Sheriff. Morning after morning thereafter Tom's place was outside the window of the south-looking room in which the Sheriff wrote. Time and again, playing with his own axe and with the Sheriff's, Tom would pass the window, not a whit more eager for his master to appear than Scott was to go out. Often Sir Walter's sore physical trials made the allotted task of writing a burden ; on such days Tom had the longer wait, and sometimes, indeed, waited in vain. At other times his persistence in hanging round the window fairly coaxed the Sheriff to let the heavy task go hang. Sometimes, if he thought that time was up and that " our books " were getting too much attention, he stood and stared in at the window till Sir Walter came.

" Our books " provided him with an occupation that was little in keeping with poaching or pony-personation. He was librarian of Abbotsford, actually in full charge of the books, and did not hesitate to remonstrate with any of the household or of the guests who marked any book or disarranged the shelves. He moved about the great room in his ordinary working clothes and heavy boots, and must have presented a curious contrast to the polished and splendid bindings that Sir Walter loved.

Tom had twenty pounds a year from the Sheriff, probably a large salary a hundred years ago. His shepherd's perquisite of a certain number of sheep was worth, perhaps, as much again, and no doubt Mrs. Purdie shared in the good things of the house. Tom was much respected by the cottars and workmen because he had saved a hundred pounds, and because his fine family Bible had cost him seven pounds. Remembering these and other titles to regard, Tom developed a certain ceremoniousness that showed appreciation of his station. When he went out to fish or to hunt with any of the family or with visitors he would not on any account go in his working jacket, but made a point of changing into the green jacket which he regularly inherited from Sir Walter.

Reading the Waverley Novels Tom declared the greatest of his comforts, for whenever he was off his sleep, as sometimes happened, he had only to take up one of the novels and he was drowsy before he had read two pages. This gave much joy at Abbotsford, and Sir Walter frequently repeated the story.

Tom's prejudices were his own, and bore no taint of resemblance to his master's. There were few men whom Sir Walter admired and loved as much as Sir Adam, but Tom detested him, and lost no opportunity of dealing him sharp cuts. When Sir Walter obtained a knighthood for Adam, Tom was openly indignant. " This will take some of the shine out of *us*," he said. Skene was a great favourite, and Tom used to give him private and confidential wrinkles about salmon-fishing, " which he thought nobody knew but himself," wrote the ungrateful Skene.

Sir Walter found in him " a Scotch slovenliness which leads him to see things half-finished without pain or anxiety." This is a gift. A ploughman who can stop in the middle of a furrow ; a clerk who can endure a littered desk ; a housewife who can stop for a cup of tea while the house is topsy-turvy—and the millions of the rest of them—how quiet of mind, how vacuous, how enviable ! And Sir Walter, whose tasks were gigantic, and who could not rest when he had a job on, how he must have despised, fretted at, envied Tom, whose mind was un-hastened by anything on earth ! Consider the deaths of both of them. The contrast is the same contrast as their lives provided. Old Tom had mentioned a sore throat, but abso-lutely nothing else. He had been out the previous day with Sir Walter and had got soaked, but no attention had been paid to that small item. He rose in the morning, and whether he felt ill or well he made no complaint, but sat down, laid his elbow on the table, put his head on his hand and, absolutely in silence and without apparent pain, died. His family thought he had drowsed, and went to and fro for an hour or two before they tried to awake him. This was Tom's death, on 29th October 1829—three years before his master's. This was euthanasia, but Sir Walter's sufferings we know.

" There is a heart cold that loved me well," said Sir Walter. " I have seldom been so much shocked " ; and again, " Though I am on most occasions like Edward Bruce, who used not to make moan for others, and loved not that others should lament for him, yet on this occasion I have felt very acute sorrow. I was so much accustomed to the poor fellow that I feel as if I had lost feet and hands, so ready was he always to supply the want of either."

Tom lies in Melrose churchyard, under a stone erected by Scott. Surely never was an act of human generosity so richly rewarded as Scott's reclamation of Tom. And it would be difficult to parallel the twenty-five years of com-radeship between these two men, one a distinguished man of letters, familiar with kings and powerful men all over the world, and the other a rough peasant.

CHAPTER XII

A DAY AT ABBOTSFORD

ON a morning of spring the laird of Abbotsford and Sheriff of the county woke about six o'clock, glanced sleepily at the window, perceived daylight, and decided it was waking-time. He lay, however, for half an hour smiling and whispering to himself, because he was an author and was turning over in his mind the story he was writing. Yesterday he had got deeper into the tangle of his plot, for he was a born plunger, and he dragged himself and the characters of his stories into what seemed inextricable situations. Those morning clarities, however, always ended in solutions so happy that they surprised him much more than they surprised even his readers.

Suddenly he heaved up his great bulk and let himself as quietly as possible out of the large curtained, old-fashioned bed. His wife as usual stirred, opened her eyes and murmured sleepily :

" You can't have had half enough sleep."

" Yes, yes. I need less than you, Charlie, so lie quiet."

He was a big heavy man with a ruddy face, and he limped heavily across the room to his dressing-room. In a moment or two there was the sound of a footstep outside : one low knock at the door, but not a word from servant or master. Leisurely he opened the door and lifted his hot shaving-water.

He was rich enough to afford a valet if he chose, but he didn't choose. On that day and always he shaved himself. He dressed himself in grey-white corduroy breeches, an old green coat with a white silk cord from buttonhole to pocket, stockings and strong shoes, and bareheaded he walked down and out of doors. Five dogs of all sizes, two terriers, two greyhounds and a huge deerhound, were lying in wait for him and sprang up at him as he appeared.

9

The house, seen from the outside, was a compact building of perhaps a dozen rooms. The walls were covered with ivy, sweetbriar, some climbing roses and winter jasmine, and there was a porch of four pillars. But the original barns and other strong outbuildings of what had plainly been a farm were apparently being made the nucleus of an enlargement to be joined up with the house in due time. There was scaffolding all round, and builders' stones and material littered the ground.

Straight to the stables went the laird. It appeared that the stable doors had been on the latch all night. He went in, and a fine hunter whinnied softly as he entered.

" Daisy, man ! " he ejaculated. " It's a rare morning, and I'm sorry there's little for you to do to-day."

The horse whinnied again almost regretfully.

" Yes, Tom and I are for the woods. It's a transplanting day. The ground's dried up fine and the young larches are fair eager to be shifted."

As he spoke he was getting a basin of oats from the corn-chest. He took it to Daisy's manger, lingered for a moment to hear the horse crunch, crunch hungrily at his breakfast. Then after some more caresses he limped back to the house.

He entered, and all the dogs entered with him, a smallish room which looked right on Tweed and which already a big wood fire made inviting and warm. Clearly the laird was well served. He sat down at his desk and opened the lid. A blotting-pad with some huge sheets of paper on it was drawn forth, and for an instant his eyes rested on some old silver ornaments and what not, apparently things belonging to an elder generation and kept there for sentimental reasons. At ten minutes past seven his long feather pen was scribbling over the huge sheets, and the eternal smile on his large, soft, expressive mouth kept placid swift measure with his transcribed thoughts.

The greyhounds nosed round three times in a circle of about twenty inches and then sat down, satisfied that there were no snakes or troublesome stinging things on the carpet. The terriers sat by the fire and the big dog lay just at his feet. They were all very silent, for the household was not yet astir, and they were a wise set of dogs ; but they bore their unnatural silence with prodigious yawns, as infectious among dogs as among men.

The spring sun lifted joyously upward, and the sounds of the household gradually increased. Servants were heard moving about the passages : steps were heard outside, and once the big deerhound rose and laid a paw across his master's knee. The laird patted the paw and the head, looked at the clock and said :

" Not yet, Maida. It's over an hour till breakfast."

Maida lay down again, and the quill, unhasting but unresting, renewed its blackening of the long lines. But Maida was restless. He heard the faint sound of a broad Scotch accent outside and he rose again.

" It's Tom," murmured the laird. " He's back very early. Must have been up before me."

Maida walked sedately to the door and thumped it heavily with a paw. The laird obediently rose, opened the door and let him out. The other dogs looked expectant : one terrier came running to the door but ran back when the laird shut it.

He sat down and wrote, wrote for another solid hour. By this time he had filled six of the huge pages with his close writing. He was busy on a book called *The Antiquary*, and he was nearly finished, though to him it was not labour but amusement. Had he known shorthand he would have been a terror to his time, for people would scarcely have been able to read as much as he would have written.

A tall boy of about fifteen, lithe and robust, bounded in, without knocking.

" Good morning, papa."

" Good morning, Wat. Is there no sign of breakfast ? "

" I don't think any of the rest are up."

" This gets worse every day. Have you been out ? "

" Yes, I've been up at Huntly Burn with Joe Shillinglaw. He had been after craws since four in the morning, and I took him with me to try some of the wild pigeons."

" Joe's daft on the gun."

" He said, papa . . ."

" Well ? "

" He said he was dying to knock over a blackcock or two. He says he wouldn't poach for worlds, but he would die happy if he got a day next October with me. . . ."

" Well, well, time enough to think of all that. Joe's a good lad, so you may keep him in mind."

" Thanks, papa ; I was sure you wouldn't mind."

" Get ye upstairs now and rouse the laggards. Take a jug of water to them if they don't jump."

Out bounded the lad, laughing and threatening wild things. He left the door open and the laird looked up when he heard screams not very far off. A quarter of an hour afterwards, when the breakfast bell clanged through the house, he calmly put away his papers and locked his desk. The greyhounds, recognising the signs of what they considered the beginning of real activity (though it is clear enough that they were the end), leapt up to his shoulder and turned themselves at one bound time after time. The terriers barked loudly.

" Ay, ay. The shop's shut and we're a' our ain men for the rest of this day," said the laird. " Down, lads, down."

He walked to the dining-room with his dogs.

" This is a small *tail* for the great Macnab," said a bright girl of thirteen as he entered. She was the only person in the room, and she flung herself at papa to be kissed.

" Ay, Lady Anne. Maida's off with Tom, and Gala has a loan of three hounds. Are the rest up ? "

" Mamma and Sophia are. I won't answer for Prince Charlie."

Loud hubbub on the stair, however, announced the rest. Mamma, a rather thin, smallish lady, came in with her big son Walter, and their arms were round each other's waist. Sophia, a very sedate girl of seventeen, passed to her place, and just as everybody was seated baby Charlie entered, rubbing his eyes. The younger girl wagged a triumphant finger at him.

" I've counted the letters. I've counted them. Thirty-seven and four parcels." Both looked at two huge piles that stood by the laird's plates.

" You'd no business to count my letters," said Charlie quite crossly.

" Hm! *Your* letters! And I opened them *all*, too. You only open the ones you think may be important."

" I don't."

Maida silently walked in, and as he sat beside his master's chair his head was considerably above the level of the table. Finette, the pet spaniel of the mistress, took her station at the head of the table and every two minutes laid an appealing paw or two on her mistress's lap ; the mute appeal was invariably rewarded by a scrap large or small, and an unbiased observer would have noticed that by the time the meal was over Finette had received about four times as much food as the great Maida. The terriers and greyhounds begged promiscuously, and one black greyhound came in for much petting though for very little miscellaneous feeding at the hand of its master.

There was a scratching at the door a moment after breakfast began, and Charlie ran to open it. Entered a huge grey cat whom the children immediately began to entice with titbits. After a few morsels, however, the cat leapt on the large easy-chair beside the fire, purred for a few moments and fell asleep.

The laird was already busy eating, and though it is to be remembered that no man in the British Islands had more worthily earned breakfast, still he seemed to take particular enjoyment in his reward. He had a big plate of porridge and cream, which he ate with a silver-mounted horn spoon. Then he got two large thick slices of salmon, which he ate with toast. Coaxed by his wife he took other two slices. Thick home-cured ham and a couple of eggs followed, and by this time he had himself cut two thick slices off the big brown loaf near him. The way he buttered some oatcake that he loved was pleasant to see. He cut a slice right through the butter and laid it on the oatcake : another slice of butter, another. Then he doubled the oatcake, took a fine bite and smiled happily at Charlie, who loved to copy papa in everything, but always fell a mile behind at oatcake. Charlie had found that if he put plenty of jam on oatcake it was a quicker business altogether.

There was one slice of salmon left, and the laird asked for it. He laid it on a plate beside him and tapped the table.

The great staghound, understanding that it was meant for him, began to eat from the table as easily and carefully as his master.

By the time bacon and eggs were finished the laird had got over the worst of the famished air that he had begun with, and turned to his letters.

"Not so many as usual this morning," he murmured, as he looked at the piles.

He picked out a small parcel, undid it, looked at it and put it in his pocket : apparently he knew its appearance. Then he began on the letters.

As he ate he opened one after another, glanced at them and threw them into a waste-paper basket in which one of the terriers had gone to sleep. Now and again he put one in his pocket.

He came to one of about twelve foolscap pages, very closely written ; he read two sentences and then looked at the end.

"Abuse ! And no name," he said. "And a shilling to pay on it. But it's a pity that this creature couldn't know that all I read was the first sentence and the last. Put it in the fire, Charlie."

Charlie jumped up, took the letter and scanned the first page carefully, but Charlie was only eleven and read slowly. With reluctance he committed it to the fire.

"Here's an invitation to dinner at Yair, Charlotte. I suppose we are free ? "

"We are always free for Yair," replied his wife, with a recognisably foreign accent.

"Will you reply ? " he asked.

"No, no. My replies are like Johnnie Ballantyne's joke about my countryman's wife, the point of which I never see— 'goot, goot for notting.' I should be sure to make some slip in spelling."

A startling apparition darkened the south window. A smallish, burglarious-looking man with a big hatchet and other instruments in his belt pressed himself close against the window and yelled as loudly as he could :

"What's the order the day, Shirra ? "

"We'll transplant the larches from the nursery to Turn-again, Tom."

" It's no a day for anything o' the sort," shouted Tom and shook his fist. " Ye'll kill my larches. It's a deevil o' a spring a' thegither ; ye'd better wait a week or twa yet."

" No, no," said the Sheriff decisively. " Another week or two and we can't plant out at all."

All the others had their heads together over an item of news that Anne had started, and the Sheriff and Tom got leave to shout as they list. Tom, however, walked off rather in a pet, and the Sheriff asked mamma what was up.

" Anne swears that Wat is all afidget for the Edinburgh carrier. He is due now, and Wat is expecting his parcel."

" Expecting isn't *fidgeting*, is it ? " asked Walter. " And I mind how Anne grat for twa hours when her white dress was late of coming last hogmanay."

One of the terriers on the rug suddenly growled and looked up.

" That must be the carrier. Wee Pepper has a spite——"

But Walter was gone like a shot, and Anne's giggles followed him. Mamma, as interested as Walter himself, followed. Sophia and Anne declared that though they weren't a bit interested they were going to see what was to be seen, and Charles, privately glad of an excuse, stopped eating. The Sheriff serenely went on with brown bread, butter and jam, and the examination of his letters.

When cheers rang through the house Charles edged off his chair and departed. Leaps and bounds on the stairs signified more excitement, and the Sheriff smiled to himself.

A quarter of an hour later there was a quiet bustle on the stair, but never a voice. The dining-room door was suddenly flung open and a tall young yeomanry lieutenant in gorgeous uniform, busbyed, booted and spurred, marched in, and solemnly strode round the table. The Sheriff was electrified. His heavy face took on the expression his friends loved, an illumination of eyes and mouth,—almost of the texture of his skin. He started up, caught the young lieutenant to his breast and kissed him.

" Son ! " he said. " You are a man. I thought you were still my little boy, but I was wrong. You are a man."

The flush of youthful triumph on Walter's face was his only

reply; that and an unaccustomed hug of his father, which was to give the Sheriff queer thrills for a week. Mamma was radiant; Charles was positively open-mouthed; Sophia looked as if she had found an elder instead of a younger brother, and Anne was awed. Could this be Wat? He looked like the beaux that Sophia talked of for ever; and if Sophia's face was an index, he was something more superb than the average.

"How do you like him, papa?" asked Wat's mother.

"You give me queer feelings, Wat. It's strange to have a big cavalryman for a son all of a sudden. Yes, the uniform is splendid. It takes something to open our eyes, but the uniform has done it. We'll have to be thinking soon what we're to do with you."

Sophia expressed her admiration, and Anne looked hers. Mamma examined everything critically, as though she had expected it to be just so, and was only concerned to see that the materials were right. At length they moved off to the hall. The bustle had awakened the grey cat and he had walked with a long, stately stride to a chair immediately beside the door, apparently another favourite seat. The gigantic Maida passed out and the grey cat coolly gave him a soft clout on the head as he passed. A shake of the head was the only response. Hamlet, the black greyhound, followed and received the same mark of authority or contempt. Even the terriers, to reach whom the cat had to claw himself tight and lean down over the chair, got each a cuff on the head from the almost human cat.

The Sheriff's woodland apparatus was lying on the hall table; he put it on—a belt containing a hatchet, a small saw and a chisel—and they all stepped outside.

The apparition of the window, Tom Purdie, was standing on the gravel holding a cob. He glanced at the party and turned his attention to bringing the cob round towards the leaping-stone near the door so that the Sheriff might mount at ease, because though he was still good enough in the saddle the Sheriff's weight and lame foot rendered mounting a matter requiring some care.

"Wha's the officer?" whispered Tom in a terribly con-spiratorial voice to Anne, and Anne found relief in a shriek of laughter. Tom gazed at her and at the officer, whose busby had changed the appearance, besides hiding a good deal of his face.

" He doesn't know him," shouted Anne. " He doesn't know him," and the whole excited family joined in the laugh against Tom.

Tom in disgust at himself took off his cap and flung it on the ground just as the Sheriff was mounting, but luckily the cob was the most reliable mount in Selkirkshire and only backed a step.

" Weel, efter that——" said Tom and grinned, showing his big white teeth.

" Isn't he a man, Tom ? " asked the Sheriff.

" He is that. We'll hae to drink his health——"

" In the evening, Tom ; in the evening," said the Sheriff lightly, for he knew Tom.

" He'll die of vanity before evening," said Anne, who was recovering from her awe.

After some happy teasing the Sheriff moved off and passed through the gate into the road. Tom walked by the horse's head and their conversation was of Walter and what a clever boy he was. Tom related wonderful stories of Walter's hits with the gun, and the Sheriff smiled his joyous smile, for though he did not quite believe all Tom's stories he did honour to Tom's circumstantial and lifelike rendering.

They trudged along the road for half a mile till they came to a turnpike-gate with a little house beside it, rather tumble-down in appearance. A sign-post showed that it was a public-house, and a large slab of stone that had carefully carved on it the dues for carriages going full and returning empty, with two horses or with eight, and a whole chapter of other extortionate charges, indicated that it was also the turnpike-keeper's house. Tom shouted at the open door and a slatternly girl appeared, took from him a small brown parcel tied with tape, and answered the Sheriff's hearty good morning with a curtsey and a smile. The parcel contained the MSS of chapters xxx., xxxi. and xxxii. of *The Antiquary*, with the revised proof-sheets of four previous chapters received the day before and checked overnight. And a hundred thousand educated people in the British Islands were dying to know whether the laird of Abbotsford really was the author of the novels that Constable was publishing, or whether he kept a dozen men writing them. A sovereign to the slattern would easily have procured any one of the hundred thousand a look inside the parcel.

The Sheriff and Tom turned aside from the highway by a cart road, and soon found themselves among the heather. Here Tom took the bridle and guided the cob carefully, for the way was heavy and dangerous.

" It's going to be a grand spring for the trees after all, Tom, I'm thinking."

" Ye may say that, Shirra. It looks better enow than it did."

" I think the young trees are growing as fast as the walls of Abbotsford, Tom."

" Ye may say that, Shirra. Ye may say that. But what would Adam Paterson say gin he heard ye ? "

" Adam's a good foreman, but masons of all men except lovers linger most ere they depart."

" Ay, and what o' them that linger in the public ? "

" Or at the side of a wall, or in the anteroom of a politician who has places to give away ? Let us respect ourselves that are happiest when we are busy, Tom."

In a few moments the cob and Tom came within sight of a squad of foresters and agricultural labourers. Two carts had come by another rough road with young larches taken from the nursery, and were vanishing homeward again. The men looked up joyously as the master appeared, and Tom's nostrils swelled with pride when the great grip of the Sheriff clutched his shoulder to descend.

The men had dug deep holes with the spade at short distances from each other, and while some of them set about making a path that Tom and he had traced some days before, the Sheriff was soon busy planting. With his own hands he planted every tree, set the roots carefully apart in the direction in which they were to grow, and steadied the stem, trampled carefully as the men filled up the hole, and lingered over each. The act of planting was all his own, and he did about fifty an hour.

" It goes to my heart to think that more than two out of three of these noble fellows will have the axe at their necks in a year or two."

" Ye canna hae't otherways, Shirra," said Tom. " Turneeps and trees, it's fair destruction till them baith if they're no thinned."

" But no man alive ever wasted sympathy on the neeps, Tom, and I daresay there isna a forester in braid Scotland ever thinned a larch planting without remorse in his heart."

The workmen joined in the discussion with many stories of the affection of men for the things of the soil. The bright breezy day crept on : the workmen stopped for an hour at midday to eat and rest, but the laird drank a long draught of buttermilk brought by a servant from the house, and ate nothing. The fever of planting, the one greatest passion of his mature manhood, took the place of meat and drink with him. He wrought with endless delight, though his lameness was a constant hindrance to his work.

During the long hours of labour the dogs were as busy as the men. They nosed, whined and howled with baffled anger after rabbits : they started a hare and had a rare skirmish, while the Sheriff laughed joyously, seeing the terriers scampering at four miles an hour after the hare and the greyhounds who careered at the rate of twenty-five. Once, when all the dogs were out of sight, and on a ridge near by a flock of sheep appeared running swiftly, Tom murmured something to the laird, who drew from the pocket of his green jacket the whistle that was tied with white cord to a buttonhole. On this he blew a thin long blast and in a moment the bounding dogs were seen on the ridge. One of the labourers was sent to investigate, for to have sheep killed by greyhounds was not unknown at Abbotsford, but after a thorough search he declared that the dogs had done no mischief.

At six o'clock the laird stopped work.

" John, you're the man in whose arithmetic I have most trust. Will you count the larches ? "

John Winnos gravely walked down the long strip that marked the day's work, and returned.

" I make it four hunder all but one," he said.

" Now," said the Sheriff, " I wouldn't have stopped under four hundred for anything, and I counted four hundred and one. Try again."

Laughter, which was never far off when the Sheriff was about, rippled round the workmen who were gathering up their tools and putting on coats. Several of the younger men eagerly ran to count for themselves.

" Four hunder and ane it is," was the cry of half a dozen, and the Sheriff looked pleased.

" There were twa out of the line in that hollow," explained John Winnos, the sub-oracle of Abbotsford.

" Right, John ; they were out of your sight at the moment. Now, lads, we're for home, and any or all of you that aren't in a great hurry home are welcome to go down to Tom's house for supper. I'll be surprised if at this very moment some roast and stew and salmon and things like that arena going from the kitchen in the direction of the cottage."

There was no cheer nor yet any speech from the reserved workmen, but frank smiles and nods of joy gave evidence of their satisfaction. A long day with the Sheriff always did end up so, and there were oftener the materials of a banquet than of a mere supper.

The Sheriff mounted his cob and Tom again took the bridle. This time they had a path all the way home.

When the Sheriff came in to dinner dressed all in black, with his hair that had been rough all day now combed and sleek, he found along with his own family, all very sedate in the presence of strangers, a couple of Frenchmen come to pay, as they said, their homage to his distinguished genius. It appeared, as dinner unloosed their tongues, that they knew *The Lady of the Lake* in opera, and that they had read neither novels nor poems in the original or in transla-tions. The Sheriff sighed deeply while with the blandest face he could put on he received their profuse praises of his exquisite genius. Dinner was nearly over, however, before he finally escaped from the topic and succeeded in devoting himself to the Earl of Buchan, who also had come across to see him and had stayed, unasked, to dinner. The earl was

owner of Dryburgh estate and of the abbey ruin, in which
was the burial-place of the Sheriff's family.

" Have you been in Edinburgh lately, my lord ? " asked
the Sheriff.

" Hem ! Yes. I was there for two days last week, and I
think I have left a mark behind me. I made up my mind
that that young painter-chiel Wilkie was worth encouraging.
I find his groups and, as we say, *genre* paintings very original.
So, happening to meet him I spoke to him and we took three
turns of Princes Street thegither. We met Strang the goldsmith, and Fraser the big grocery man, and anither eediot
they call Wilson—he has three of Raeburn's portraits—and I
took particular heed to stop and introduce Wilkie to them."

He looked complacently at his plate.

" No doubt," said the Sheriff " it may do Wilkie some good
in the future."

" May ? " exclaimed the earl. " His fortune's made. To
be seen with the Earl of Buchan in Princes Street is, though I
say it myself, better than pride of place at the Academy. The
haill three are aye at me for advice afore they buy a single
picture, and they buy a heap mair than ever I could afford to
buy. Wilkie's all right now. He'll hae commissions frae the
three of them, and the public 'll follow like sheep."

" You must feel like Mæcenas re-arisen."

" Ha, ha ! Maybe, Shirra, maybe. But to-night I am mair
in the mood of Achilles preparing for the funeral games of
Patroklos. I was in the auld abbey on Monday, and I was
studying your burying-ground. It gave me the notion that
you would like me to undertake the arrangement of your
burial, should I outlive you——"

" Dieu ! " said the Sheriff's wife, and then whispered to
Sophia, " It is true, then, as half the world says. The man *is*
mad."

" I don't think he is," whispered Sophia, " but just one
thick stick of conceit."

" —It will be an important event, of course, for no doubt
the carriages of half the nobility of Scotland will be there.
So I have spent the last two days drawing out a plan for the
occasion and I have it here——"

He drew out a packet and unfolded it ; it appeared to be several foolscap sheets pasted longwise to make one long strip.

" I have put the procession down in the order I think it should go, and I have arranged a time-table of the proceedings. So I wish you would look over it.   I may say that I'll readily fall in with any suggestions you care to make, as you are in a way the person whose wishes ought to be considered."

During this harangue the Sheriff's face was a study.   At first in sheer astonishment and anger his shaggy eyebrows had dipped deep over his steady blue eyes, almost obscuring them, but after glancing round the table and seeing the mute horror of every one, he listened with growing joy.   The big expressive mouth smiled, laughed : his eyes danced : he leant back in his chair, and as the earl handed him the paper he burst into Berserker roars of laughter.   The rest of the family then saw the joke too, and laughed uproariously.

The earl's face flushed.

" This is not good taste," he said.   " Surely the subject is not a matter for laughter."

" You must forgive me, my lord," said the Sheriff through his tears.   " It is inexcusable, ill-bred.   Nobody ought to treat such a serious matter in such a ghastly style ; but your well-known sensitiveness will forgive me.   So this is the time-table. Yes. . . .   ' Chief pall-bearer, the Right Honourable David, Earl of Buchan.'   Yes, yes.   ' From 2.30 to 3 p.m. an eulogy of the deceased by the Right Honourable David, Earl of Buchan.'   Yes, yes, I see.   ' Entertainment of guests at Abbotsford.   The Right Honourable David, Earl of Buchan, will receive the guests.'   Very satisfactory indeed.   ' A solemn toast to the undying greatness—imphm—by, of course, the Right Honourable David, Earl of Buchan.' "

" My lord, I am overcome by your kindness, positively overcome.   (A bow from the earl.)   I cannot find words in which to express my sensations.   (Again the earl bowed.) I certainly consider this a unique tribute (the earl bowed very gravely), and I shall examine the document very carefully."

He put it in his hip pocket, and the earl looked a trifle disappointed.

" Meantime, mamma, if you will allow us, we shall accompany you when you leave the table, and Sophia will sing *all* her songs to his lordship, so as to drive away the melancholy thoughts that must be associated with such a subject as he has had to devote himself to for the past few days."

NOTE.—The actual incident was a good deal more cold-blooded than this account of it. It was while Scott was suffering agonies of cramp in the stomach, pain that would have killed fifty ordinary men, that this nobleman came to assure him of his interest in the forthcoming funeral. Luckily he was intercepted, but only after violence. James Ballantyne was sent to apologise, and learned the full extent of the earl's solicitude.

CHAPTER XIII

THE BALLANTYNES AND THE BUSINESSES

AN enormous part of Sir Walter's lifework, income, time and worry was connected with his ventures as partner in a printing firm and partner in a publishing firm. When he began to publish books, sold his copyrights and noted how much of the profits of a successful book adhered to the publishers and printers, he asked himself why he should not share the business profits. His capital and his enormous energy supplied the answer, and he found in James Ballantyne an agent that suited him perfectly.

When Scott as a boy of twelve spent some weeks recuperating at Kelso he attended school there, and grew familiar with James. They met again in manhood when James was a solicitor in his spare time and for an occupation was editor of a provincial weekly paper, for the law was no more a success for him than for Scott. James was then and always small and stout and pompous, black-bearded, with a theatrical air that he got from actors, among whom he lived and moved. He prided himself on being a John Bull, was keen on large roasts, on ale and whisky and the indulgent respectable side of life generally. He fitted well the name of Fatsman, which Scott the inveterate nicknamer had given him. He sang well and heartily, interpreting the heavier of Sir Walter's songs, the political squibs, with great success. He was dark and excitable ; one of his eyebrows frowned over its eye, and the other pushed itself up at an angle. In the judgment of all who knew him he was an honest man. Scott never spoke a word of disillusionment in James, even when the crash came and the foundations of their partnership were torn up and exposed to minute examination. But though truthful and direct, James had so theatrical a voice and gesture, and was altogether so affected, that Lockhart while testifying to his honesty says that his manner was apt to give strangers the impression that he was insincere.

When Scott renewed his acquaintance with Ballantyne they were both about twenty-five, and Scott began to cast about for a means of making himself useful to his old chum, and incidentally of making Ballantyne useful to him. Ballantyne had printing presses, and loved a well-printed page and a fine binding. Accordingly in 1799 Scott offered him the printing of " a volume of Border Ballads " that in due time was to blossom into the seven volumes of *The Minstrelsy of the Scottish Border*. In April 1802 he was urging Ballantyne to come and set up as a printer in Edinburgh, promising him a share in the printing of law process-papers, and offering to lend him money to enable him to do so. Ballantyne was not loth to drop his profession, and by the end of the same year he had accepted a loan from Scott and had removed from Kelso to Abbeyhill, Edinburgh.

It was early in 1805 when, after the publication of *The Lay of the Last Minstrel*, success in literature was assured, that Scott made the blunder of his life. He had six or seven thousand pounds, a legacy from his Uncle Robert, and *The Lay* had brought him fame, with the assurance of a career.

He had two courses in his mind. One was to buy the little estate of Broadmeadows on the northern bank of the Yarrow, and many a time he rode round it with desire in his eyes, but in the end he denied himself the pleasure of becoming a laird.

The course he took with his capital was the beginning of the troubles that drove him to loss, infernal worry, and premature death. James Ballantyne applied to him for a second loan, and Scott, who seems to have had this end in view for years, refused a loan, but offered to pay money down for a third share in Ballantyne's business. James agreed like a shot, and Scott paid over his money and his life.

By April 1805 Scott had entered into the spirit of business and was full of great schemes for printing and publishing. He suggested that Ballantyne should propose to certain publishers the printing of the British poets in at least a hundred volumes, and offered to edit them for thirty guineas a volume—at least three thousand guineas for the whole edition. His third share in the business of printing would, of course, have provided more. This design ultimately fell through, but many others took its place, and he took care to secure a share of printing as well as of publishing profits by insisting that whatever he wrote or edited must be printed by his own firm. He never made it known, however, that he was a partner.

It was Scott who decided what books the firm of James Ballantyne & Co. were to deal with, and he appears to have undertaken a general superintendence of the books printed by the firm. This must have given him a great deal of labour. It was in this year of great schemes, too, that he began *Waverley* and on Erskine's advice put it aside. How he must afterwards have regretted that he let it lie for nine years ! for he lost not only that success, but the successes that would have followed it.

It was in or about 1808 that John Ballantyne, the younger brother of James, after a series of adventures in tailoring and shopkeeping, clerking as a cashier in London, marrying (apparently the least satisfactory adventure of all), and acquiring the pleasant habits of heavy drinking and loose living, came to Edinburgh as a clerk in the firm of James Ballantyne & Co. at £200 a year.

He was small, but quick and courageous, infinitely merry, quaint in his expressions, fond of sport and exercise, and in a short time he wound himself round the heart of heavy, good-humoured Walter Scott. His voice was high and harsh, the right instrument for grotesque merriment ; he had an astounding gift of acting ; was very thin, and hopped with a peculiar jumping walk. To the Sheriff, who delighted in originality, John was an oasis in the desert of social life.

In 1808, the year of John's arrival, Scott and the Ballantynes began to have disputes and differences with Archibald Constable the publisher, who was the chief support of the Ballantyne press. Constable was the publisher of the *Edinburgh Review*, and its notice of *Marmion* and many of its political articles had wounded and offended Sir Walter. John Murray in London, thinking over the problems of publishing, realised this, and had insight and information enough to concentrate on the Ballantynes. James Ballantyne and Murray met in Yorkshire and exchanged views; apparently James was ready to suggest the creation of a publishing business in Edinburgh, and Murray was ready with the London alliance which was necessary for success. In October, John Murray arrived at Ashestiel, to find that over an article on Spain in the *Edinburgh Review* Scott had cancelled his subscription. Constable himself wrote against Scott's name on the original list of subscribers "Stopt," and added three marks of indignation—! ! !

The Lord Advocate, after communicating with Canning, pressed Scott to become editor of a new Review, expressly designed to disseminate the opinions of the Government; but Sir Walter did not feel inclined to sacrifice his Clerkship of Session, his residence in Scotland, and a dozen other advantages for the responsibilities of political controversy. Ultimately Gifford was chosen; Murray was ready to undertake the publishing; Canning on behalf of the Government promised confidential information, and so the *Quarterly Review* was founded.

These alliances and connections strengthened Scott's determination. He had found it easy to become a partner in a printing firm; his quarrels with Constable's partner and with Constable's publications inclined him to set up a publishing business as well, and Lockhart suggests that John Ballantyne played many tricks in order to induce Scott to do so. With such a sanguine and energetic nature as Sir Walter's behind it there was no time lost, for in December 1808 the publishing firm of John Ballantyne & Co. was established in Hanover Street, Edinburgh. Scott supplied one-half of the capital, and each of the Ballantynes supplied a quarter. Lockhart says that Scott appears to have provided James's quarter, and rather inclines to suggest that he provided John's as well; but these are assumptions. By the establishment of the *Quarterly* he had paid Jeffrey and Constable the "flap with a fox-tail" that he owed the reviewer of *Marmion*. In the launch of his publishing firm he exulted because it would "avenge certain impertinences which in the vehemence of their whiggery Constable & Co. had indulged in" towards him. He referred, as we have recorded, not to Constable, but to Hunter, the partner. About this time he mentioned James Ballantyne as the celebrated Ballantyne, and was proud to tell all concerned that the publishing firm had been equipped with a long purse and a sound political creed.

In these arrangements there were all the foundations of solid success, but there were various flaws in the personalities concerned. In the first place it is strange that Scott, who determined what books the publishing firm was to accept for publication, loaded his firm with the most unsaleable books of that generation. " I like well Walter Scott's *ain bairns*," said Constable, the wit, long before, " but heaven preserve me from his adoptions ! " Scott was not to be warned. As early as 1810 James wrote him that Weber's edition of Beaumont and Fletcher, published by John Ballantyne & Co., was going to be a failure. Weber was one of Scott's amanuenses, and his labours had been published because Sir Walter did not like to say no. A series of the poets was also a failure. A *History of the Culdees*, by an old doctor of divinity who was a friend of Scott's, was a heavy loss, and *The Annual Register*, a pet creation of Scott's own, was an annual anxiety, a disappointment, and a loss of £1000 a year.

The other side of the counter is more attractive. *The Lady of the Lake*, one of Scott's *ain bairns*, was sold at two guineas when it appeared. Scott parted with the copyright to the firm of John Ballantyne & Co. (himself and the two brothers) for £2000, but apart from that he got a share of the profits of the publishing firm and a share of the profits of the printing firm. On these terms most of his own books were issued for many years, and as there were twenty thousand copies of *The Lady of the Lake* sold in the year of publication the profits must have been large. On those profits, however, the Ballantynes and Scott lived without much balancing of books, and " the large sums received never formed an addition to capital, but were expended by the partners," who also borrowed freely on the security of the businesses. The failures, however, had to be paid for. It was Sir Walter's successful editions of Swift and Dryden, his volumes of Sadleir and Somers, and many other heavy tasks, that brought most of these failures to the firm of John Ballantyne & Co. These editions gave employment to several hacks who, by Scott's influence, got some of their own dry-as-dust productions published by Ballantyne and even by Constable, who grew so bitterly aphoristic about them. As the books of such men were often of some antiquarian interest they appealed to Sir Walter on his kindliest side, but as they were seldom of a nature that appealed to the buyers of books they were mostly complete failures, and the failures reacted on the profits of Scott, Constable and the two Ballantynes in a way that no doubt helped to keep the floating debts of all the firms larger than they would have been had Sir Walter refused to publish them. In this way the obscure people whom Sir Walter helped had their share in creating the catastrophe of 1826.

A second flaw was the rather careless business habits of James Ballantyne, who had never had any training whatsoever as a master printer. He had begun with a newspaper, had been befriended into a good law and general printing business, and took everything seriously except minding the shop and the accounts.

Another flaw was the character of John Ballantyne. He was full of cunning subtleties ; he was impudent and yet subservient. He wrote about Scott to Constable—" He has taken it into his green jacket and old hat to," etc., but when he was made the subject of jokes Scott laughed uproariously at him and no offence could be taken. Scott nicknamed him Rigdumfunnidos, Rigdum for short, and he accepted it jauntily, while his elder brother was horrified when he heard of Aldiborontiphoscophornio, Scott's rather malicious pomposity of a nickname for him. Both names were taken from a forgotten book of Carey's.

John was eternally active and obliging in Scott's affairs. When he was asked to do anything, from scouring London, Paris and Brussels for an article of vertu, to transcribing the novels with his own hand, in order to conceal Scott's authorship ; from selecting young Walter's equipment to obliging Scott's guests with mimicry better than that of the best professional actors, John did it as it ought to be done, wholeheartedly, and in a style that no other person could approach.

But he was certainly a dangerous business companion,

and only Sir Walter's supreme confidence in himself and in his own honour could have sustained the practices and tricks of such a man. One of his habits, of which Scott often complained, was that when leaving Abbotsford or Castle Street he " slipt away like a knotless thread." Scott continually had to lecture him about full and frank statements of the money matters of the firms, and as moments of parting are always moments of definite instruction John Ballantyne shirked them.

James had some taste in literature, and it was not long till it was an understood thing that he as well as Erskine should criticise the proofs of Scott's verses. When Sir Walter took to novel-writing he dashed off the volumes so swiftly that he depended greatly on James, and at times on John, to point out errors, anachronisms, blunders of various kinds, which it is almost impossible for any author on any subject entirely to escape, even taking time and care.

In 1810 Scott resurrected the first third of *Waverley*, condemned by Erskine in 1805, and sent it to James for his opinion. Ballantyne criticised, and was rather inclined to praise it, but it was held back for a further period of two or three years. " The language is spirited, but perhaps rather careless," wrote Ballantyne, a good description of Scott's style, given at a day's notice, and with little of the material available to us.

Meantime the publishing business went from proud hope to bottomless confusion. The books that it published would not sell ; the retail bookshops would not have them, and the public would not buy them. John Ballantyne had not the remotest notion either of a publisher's business or of the public taste in books, and neither James nor Scott could help him. Constable regarded their flounderings with friendly anxiety and contempt. He liked " jocund Johnnie," and he admired Scott so much that he asked for nothing better than Sir Walter's countenance. In 1813 Scott made up his quarrel with Constable in order to get him to take over part of the stock of many unsaleable books, for by that time, less than five years after the establishment of the publishing business, it was notorious in the trade that the firm of John Ballantyne & Co. was a disaster. It was even rumoured that it was bankrupt.

As worries accumulated on Scott's head he continually

besought John not to conceal the facts. Time and again
John put statements of current debts, bills and assets before
him ; time and again they were falsified, and Scott was summoned from drawing-rooms and receptions to interview
messengers carrying bills that had to be met the next day.
Time and again he expostulated with John. One marvels
that he did not then or afterwards get rid of him. Johnnie
apparently could do what he liked with the Sheriff, and in
face of the provocation, worry, almost anguish that these
business methods gave to Scott I cannot understand why he
did not take warning and cut the whole connection. The
only conclusion I can come to is that his purchases of land
and his building, carried out not with cash but always in
anticipation, with bills on the banks, rendered a business
security essential.

Bills flew about in astonishing numbers, and the accumula-
tion of them was much more than Scott could pay, so he had to
resort to renewals and new borrowings to meet his liabilities.
At times he was in utter despair. " God's will be done ! "
he wrote to Constable. " There will be enough of property,
including my private fortune, to pay every claim."

This was in 1813. Madness to go on thereafter in the
same fashion, laying up continual worry and inevitable disaster
for himself ! But he took absolutely no warning, though at
length the firm of John Ballantyne & Co. came to an end.
Possibly Scott regarded the troubles of 1813, the alarm of the
banks and the failures of his publishing house, as unlikely to
recur, because 1813 was the crisis of the Napoleonic wars,
when credit was restricted for the final strain and when in other
ways trade was in a disorganised state. It was a good thing
that the publishing firm was dissolved before the slack credits
that were made possible after Waterloo came round, for if
that firm had struggled through till 1826, John Ballantyne's
methods and Sir Walter's land hunger would have accumulated bills enough to have ruined Scott five times over.

His own ways were astonishing. In mid-May 1813 he
moved heaven and earth to save himself from bankruptcy,
and in June—the very next month—he was hot on the hunt
for a new lairdship to join to Abbotsford. In July of that

year he actually bought Cauldshiels loch and a tract of land. He had tried to raise the purchase price from Constable on the strength of the unwritten *Lord of the Isles*, but had failed. It is reasonable to assume that he raised the money on the promise to pay of James Ballantyne & Co., or even of John Ballantyne & Co., or of both.

His difficulties that year were cleared up by getting the Duke of Buccleuch to guarantee £4000.

" For the first time these many weeks I shall lay my head on a quiet pillow," he said in mid-May 1813. He had put every available guinea and more into Abbotsford, and he had had to find money somewhere. Besides the Duke's £4000 he had received £2000 cash from Constable for the unsaleable books, and he persisted in thinking that " The Crafty " had got a good bargain; but Constable ultimately had to sell this stock, and more that Scott and Ballantyne palmed off on him by the same method in future years, at a half and a third of what he paid for it.

It was while he was harassed by these bills, by the incapacity of the Ballantynes, by the dread of bankruptcy and dishonour, that he thought again of the manuscript of *Waverley*. He took it out, read what he had written, thought it had been undervalued by Erskine, and sat down to it. In three weeks he wrote the two-thirds necessary to complete it.

So at the moment of despair he constructed the foundation of a new fortune.

A few months afterwards Charles Erskine, his own Sheriff-substitute, asked for repayment of a loan that he had advanced to James Ballantyne & Co., and Scott wrote *Guy Mannering* in six weeks, in order to pay this debt of honour.

Constable was a generous and ready helper in all Scott's troubles. Not only did he take over large quantities of unsaleable books, but he persuaded other publishers to help in the same way—and his reward was Scott's conviction that he got great bargains. The bills also, that were afterwards to ruin Scott, were backed by Constable, whose assistance, though it became part of the disaster, was considered a providence when it was asked for and given.

As the publishing business still dragged itself along, Scott reluctantly decided to lay the whole case of the firm before Constable for his advice. There could be only one decision, and it appears to have been taken, but I cannot give the date when the publishing firm definitely ceased to exist. By a trick to be described later, Johnnie succeeded in 1818 in palming off the last and most of his books on Constable, and he himself returned to the printing firm as cashier, with an interest, at Constable's expense, in all future Waverley Novels.

Constable was so eager to publish those novels that he accepted them on any terms. He usually agreed that Scott and he should share the profits equally, but at least in the cases of *Rob Roy* and *Kenilworth* it is on record that Scott allowed Constable only one-third of the profits, and insisted that the other sixth of the publishing profits should be handed over—not to himself, but to John Ballantyne. Thus for doing absolutely nothing John got £1200 out of *Rob Roy* and a great deal out of *Kenilworth*. Apparently Scott handed over a sixth of the profits of every novel in the same way.

CHAPTER XIV

THE BALLANTYNES AND THE BUSINESSES—*continued*

THE most rejoicing years of Scott were from 1814 till 1819. In the latter year his health definitely broke, and his supreme physical happiness utterly gave way; but in those years he was happy acquiring land, planting it, building his great house, decorating and furnishing it, and receiving visitors with an open hand and heart. It is pleasant to pause and watch him during those joyous years, and it is to be remembered that in those years the Ballantynes were not only his tradesmen, but were his friends and companions. Every day for half a lifetime Scott walked home from the law-courts by way of Ballantyne's printing-house in the Canongate, or of the office near by. He took the old coach up the Mound in the morning, but the way down was easier and there was less hurry in the afternoon. Ballantyne as often as not had some other publisher or some actor or literary friend in, expecting Scott to call, and laughter was the invariable result of a meeting, no matter how many worries lay on the heads of all.

In 1818 James Ballantyne lived in St. John Street, a row of substantial old-fashioned houses between the Canongate and Holyrood Road, not far from the printing-shop. The entrance from the Canongate is through a pend or close, a mere gateway below houses, and it is rather startling to come out of the confined Canongate and to see the rough bulk of Salisbury Crags looming over St. John Street. James's house, like so many that endure in Edinburgh, had a basement storey; at the front it stood beside the pavement and behind it had a small walled-in green.

Some years previous to this time Ballantyne had married the daughter of a prosperous Berwickshire farmer, and he had now a family of five children. His father and mother had been inmates of his house for years, and he was as exemplary a son as he was a good husband and father. With his family, and even when entertaining a few friends, he was content to be a natural man, but there were festivities at which he felt that he must rise to the historic occasion.

When any publication of importance was about to be issued, especially if it was a Waverley Novel, James gave a dinner in honour of the event. Scott was always there, and in their day Erskine, the Duke of Buccleuch, Lockhart, and other intimates were usually present. There was also a crowd of James's own literary allies, singers, theatrical people and others.

Turtle and venison, iced punch, strong beer, and sherry were James's favourite items. When dinner was over he gave three toasts, first " the general joy of the whole table," then the King, and then the health of Walter Scott. After some conversation and drinking James rose once more, every vein on his brow distended, his eyes solemnly fixed on vacancy, to propose, not as before in his stentorian key but with bated breath, in the sort of whisper by which a stage conspirator thrills the gallery—" Gentlemen, a bumper to the immortal author of *Waverley* ! " At this there was always great cheering, in which Scott joined. The name of the new novel was announced, and they drank to its success.

Then James, who liked to hear his own voice, sang, and sang well, the ballads of the time. Other singers followed, for he usually got the best professional singers of Edinburgh to dine on such occasions, and his own singing was not bettered by any. Other toasts were drunk, and at length the more ornamental guests withdrew and James got scope. " Claret and olives made way for broiled bones and a mighty bowl of punch, and when a few glasses of the hot beverage had restored his powers James opened with a sonorous voice on the merits of the new novel. ' One chapter, one chapter only,' was the cry. After ' Nay, by our Lady, nay,' and a few more coy shifts the proof sheets were at length produced, and James read aloud the most striking dialogues."

He read with fine emphasis and understanding, and made a strong impression on his hearers. " One bumper more to Jedediah Cleishbotham ! " shouted the exultant James as he ended, and then he sang the final song of the evening, which was always "The Last Words of Marmion."

Whoever else enjoyed these dinners it is clear that James did; they were his memorable events, and though Lockhart succeeds in making James somewhat ridiculous, he is compelled to do justice to Ballantyne's powers. He was, in fact, a prominent business man with good taste in literature and some proficience in art. Of much inferior men Lords Provosts (who are created baronets) have been made.

The physical and mental contrast between James and John Ballantyne was a source of amusement to Scott all his days, and it was indeed strange, for except that both were on the small side they were as different in shape, habits, mind, pleasures and conversation as any two men could be.

John lived at Trinity, in a house that stood in its own grounds, and which though, or perhaps because, he fought with his wife he had named Harmony Hall. The gardens had many shady corners, trellised alleys and mysterious bowers among bright borders, and often there were joyous guests adorning them too. The sitting-rooms opened on perfumed conservatories, and the rooms were furnished with articles picked up in Brussels or Paris, for after 1814, though the publishing business was still nominally in existence, John set up as an auctioneer of expensive articles—a scheme suggested by the capable Constable, who knew John's powers better than he himself did. For the auction-room John scoured the Continent.

In his villa was a private wing, and the doors or openings into it had been constructed for the express purpose of keeping his wife out. They were only a few inches wide, so that Mrs. John, who was stout, never saw the inside of that portion of the building. It may be assumed that a man who to annoy his unoffending wife could carry out and perpetuate a plan of that kind without shame would not stick at a trifle in his dealings with men.

"His dinners were in all respects Parisian. . . . The piquant pasty of Strasburg or Perigord was never to seek, and even the *pièce de résistance* was probably a boar's head from Coblenz or a turkey, ready stuffed with truffles, from the Palais Royal. The pictures scattered among John's innumerable mirrors were chiefly of theatrical subjects, many of them portraits of beautiful actresses." He was even a greater entertainer of entertainers than his brother was.

He had a well-filled stable, and followed the foxhounds when he could. When he drove he took out a bright blue dog-cart with a prancing pair of highstrung horses, tandem, and on occasion he tooted the French horn as he drove, scorning to take thought of the weakness of his lungs. His horses were all called after heroes in Scott's poems or novels, and about 1818 he usually arrived at his auction-room on a tall milk-white hunter called Old Mortality. (How, by the way, did he address the horse in those friendly moments when a man calls to his beast ?) He rode up from Leith attended by a leash of grey-hounds who also had their names from the novels. He dressed in a light grey frock-coat, with emblems of the chase on its silver buttons, in white cord breeches and jockey boots. Scott went to John's saleroom nearly every day, and Maida knew this so well that he often trotted along to Hanover Street and couched among the greyhounds just about the time the Sheriff was likely to be coming from court.

He was full of the most extraordinary stories, usually exaggerations of actual facts. Quaint and ludicrous touches fermented in his mind, and he produced them at length as masterpieces of dialogue or recital that furnished many a first-rate comedian with the best of his creations. He had an extremely self-centred manner, but was in grain an adapter of himself. He was at his best and funniest with Constable the generous and proud of heart, who sincerely liked him and associated with him a great deal ; but though Constable was as open as the sun, continually helpful and kind, John Ballantyne was incapable of responding.

On the evening of 5th May 1817, a beautiful day, Constable, Scott and John Ballantyne had come to an agreement about the proposed novel of *Rob Roy*, out of which the entirely super-fluous John was to get £1200. After dinner they went outside, and John in high spirits asked if he could have Rob's gun out so as to let off a " few de joy," as he called it. " Johnnie, my man," said Constable, " what puts drawing at sight into *your* head ? " Scott rang a peal of laughter at the insinuation, and then to soothe him called for " The Cobbler of Kelso." The perfect mimic hopped on a large stone, sat cobblerwise, and began a marvellous imitation. Scott and he as boys in Kelso had often lingered at the open stall of a cobbler who had a black-bird. The cobbler talked to it and whistled to it all day, and blackie sang back. As the cobbler, Johnnie put on a hoarse cracked voice, and uttered the wildest unending endearments. The rich whistle of the blackie was done as exquisitely, and the contrast was superb. Scott invariably sat enchanted while John performed this interlude.

John swallowed Constable's direct joke in silence and with a wry face, but he paid it back in his own way with interest a year afterwards, and rejoiced to tell everybody the tale of his dex-terous trick. Scott had directed him explicitly to propose to Constable the publication of a second series of *The Tales of My Landlord* in four volumes. " I have hungered and thirsted to see the end of those shabby borrowings among friends. They have all been wiped out except the good Duke's £4000, and I will not suffer either new offers of land or anything else to come in the way of that clearance."

John casually mentioned the proposed four new volumes to Constable, conveying the impression that Scott intended to divide this second series, as he had divided the first, among Constable, Murray and Blackwood. *Blackwood's Magazine* had recently been started, and its political articles were quickly ousting Constable's *Edinburgh Review* from the favour of the public. Ballantyne cunningly argued that Constable would do a great deal to keep out Blackwood, and when Constable ex-pressed the hope that he would have the publication of the four volumes, Ballantyne said it was an indispensable condition, laid down by the author, that *all* the remaining unsaleable stock of John Ballantyne & Co. must be taken over by the publishers of the new Tales. The proud, sensitive and reckless man agreed to take the lot, and paid £5270 for it. When he finally disposed of this stock he realised one-third of what he had paid.

When his undiagnosed tuberculosis was urging him along with all manner of restless dreams, John Ballantyne planned (out of the profits of novels with which he had nothing to do) a villa at Kelso. Scott went down to look at the building, and there and then offered Johnnie as a free gift his services as editor and Life-writer of a Library of the Novelists. This meant a fortune for John, who gladly accepted it; but though some of the series appeared, it was dropped after John's death.

He died on 16th June 1821, and left Sir Walter (" the faithful creature," wrote Scott, touched by John's gratitude) the reversion of £2000 towards the completion of the library at Abbotsford. The sum was to be life-rented by his wife; but it had no existence, for he was deeply in debt when he died.

Sir Walter was greatly shaken by Johnnie's illness and death. " I feel that there will be less sunshine for me from this day forth," he said at the graveside when the sun broke through the clouds. In those later years James and John had rather quarrelled, and no wonder, considering some of John's on-goings; but the illness broke all webs, and it was in the house of kindly James that he died.

It was probably the quaint originality of Johnnie that made Scott so fond of him. In the Sheriff's eyes it did not matter whether he did evil or good. That inveterate nick-namer made names for him in all sorts of kindly contemptuous ways, called him Leein' Johnnie, and in contrast to him called John Stevenson, the chief clerk in the publishing firm, True Jock. Picaroon and Mr. Puff were other nicknames he got from Scott. John took them all as a good joke, and laughed as readily as the rest. When the publishers were nicknaming each other after kings, and Constable got the name of the Czar, he retaliated by calling Johnnie the Dey of Alljeers, and suggested (in 1812, a shrewd hit) that he was as good as dethroned.

Johnnie laughed at everything, including the Waverley Novels. He called written matter, which no doubt he was sick of looking at, good, bad or worse " abomination."

There was a third brother, Alexander, of whom Scott saw a good deal too. He was a fine player on the flageolet, was often at Abbotsford with his instrument, and was esteemed by Scott as a kindly and modest man, but he seems to have had no connection with the businesses.

In 1817 Scott and Ballantyne bought *The Edinburgh Weekly Journal*, and James became editor. He had already been for years the theatrical critic of a newspaper, and editorship itself was nothing new to him. Scott contributed many articles to this paper.

In 1818 Scott transferred all the copyrights of the Waverley Novels to Constable for £12,000, and as other novels were published two subsequent purchases of the same kind were made, involving over £10,000. These copyrights, for which Constable paid over £22,000, were bought back by Scott and Cadell in 1826 for £8500.

Scott escaped from the publishing business, and in August 1813 he did for a few days threaten to retire from the printing business as well. In 1816 he had made so many advances to the printing firm of James Ballantyne & Co. that it was wound up, and he became the sole owner, with James as manager at four hundred a year. In 1821, after five years, during which the business belonged to Scott alone, James asked Scott to take him back as a partner, and Scott then considered himself so reimbursed that he did so by a signed contract from Whitsunday 1822.

This matter raises several considerations. In the first place, during those six years Scott drew the whole profits of the business. In the second place, having full control, he must have obtained, if he had it not before, full and exact information in regard to the extent and the nature of the firm's debts. These debts must have been *his* debts, not Ballantyne's, and he must have been perfectly satisfied that Ballantyne had nothing to do with debts in the firm's name, when he showed such confidence in taking him back freely as a partner. And if during those six years the business had continued to be a trouble to him, or if by any chance it had been a loss, he had six years in which to wind it up. It is perfectly clear that he found it profitable.

It is alleged against the Ballantynes and Constable that though 1819 was high-water mark of the sales of Scott's novels, and that thereafter the sale declined, they concealed this fact from him, while in the belief that his profits were as large as ever Scott went forward with plans of building, of acquiring land, and of entertainment that made the years subsequent to 1819 the most expensive years of his life.

This I do not believe, because in 1823, when *Quentin Durward* appeared, its sale was slow till France rang with its praises. The slowness of sale was communicated from London to Constable, from Constable to Scott and to the Ballantynes, and a terrific to-do was made about the matter. It is reasonable to assume that what Scott was openly and immediately told in 1823 he was told in the three preceding years.

The spectacle of Scott and Ballantyne growing old and failing in health together is full of pathos. When Scott, struck with paralysis and no longer capable of the bright imaginations of his youth and maturity, took up the subject of Count Robert of Paris, there were plenty who could see at a glance that the master of mystery and brightness was in a cloud for ever. Not James Ballantyne. His innocent sincerity never proved itself so genuine as in his remonstrances about Count Robert. He read the sheets with annoyance, wrote time and again scolding Scott for carelessness, a bad choice of subject, too much haste, the impossible names of the characters, and other incidental points.

In fact, James's criticisms were almost brutal in their innocent force. He never dreamt that his magician was anything but careless and engaged on an unsuitable subject, but Scott was able to draw his own deductions. His family, watchful, but thwarted by his iron determination, could always tell when he had had a letter from James, because a certain twitching of the mouth, that had become habitual after the attack of February 1830, visibly increased for a while after he read certain familiar packets.

He did not worry about Ballantyne's opinion, of course, nor about the opinion of any man on earth, but to perish before his honour was redeemed !

Scott openly told Cadell that he was played out, that like Fielding and Smollett he had better go abroad and die. The publisher remonstrated, and said that it was wrong to consider himself past writing. Ballantyne's criticisms were discussed, and Scott made the pathetic admission that showed the clearness of his mind even in the cloud that encompassed him :

" I never had the least thought of blaming him, and indeed my confidence in his judgment is the most forcible part of the whole affair. It is the consciousness of his sincerity which makes me doubt whether I can proceed with the *Count Paris.*"

CHAPTER XV

SCOTT AS A LITERARY MAN

WITH the question of Scott's stature as an artist in letters we
have little to do, but it is impossible to leave out those interesting points of character and experience that are bound
up with his books.

The characteristic and the vital quality of an artist, the
fire within him that illumines his own generation, are too
easily forgotten when fifty or a hundred years have brought
his work into the cold gallery of the immortals. But we who
admire Scott will never let the appraisers of fame forget that
all literature was dull before him and he made it interesting.
The Elizabethan dramatists were as dull a set of ranters as ever
existed : the Restoration writers, with all the resources of
obscenity and viciousness, could not be humorous : the Miltons,
Popes, Swifts, Fieldings, Grays and the rest were dull and
heavy. Hacks, students, politicians, men about town, all
turning to bookmaking to pass the time, to offend, or to make
money.

And then for the first time since Shakespeare arose a man
with joyful power in the description of his fellow-creatures.
Into the literature of England Walter Scott brought enthusiasm, delight in the open air and in sports, and a living realisation
of former days that was happily due because the labours of
antiquarians had prepared the public for the romantic presentation of events and habits of old times. He put more life into
his minor characters than had ever been put by any writer of
books in England except Shakespeare, and, like Shakespeare,
he succeeded best with these minor characters. He evoked
the characteristics of Scotland, physical and national ; he
created magnificent pictures of old time like *Ivanhoe*, the
imperishable romance, and interludes with all the flavour of
former days as in *The Fortunes of Nigel*.

He made a tremendous sensation as a poet, a novelist, an antiquary, and an editor of English books of importance. It is pleasant to repeat that his poems brought the whole aristocracy of Britain to exhaust the sensations that were to be procured by obtaining views of Melrose Abbey by daylight, moonlight and candlelight, and that when those sensations were exhausted he persuaded them (by the mouth of Johnnie Bower) to take a view of it through their own legs. Then he sent them on tours of appreciation through the Highlands, a pilgrimage that the generations of men are not likely to relinquish. He changed the spirit of British history ; he gave a revelation of Scottish character that has stood the test of a hundred years and is still fresh and true. Some of his essays, little read though they may be, are much better than essays that are circulated to-day as masterpieces, and I do not believe that *Ivanhoe*, high-flown as it is, will ever grow stale.

Yet he sincerely believed that his great success in literature was due not to innate talent, but to the course of his reading and experiences as a boy, to his upbringing, and in a great measure to luck—in fact, to causes outside of himself. He jogged Moore in the ribs and congratulated Tom and himself on the fact that they had arrived before so many clever young fellows had come along with verses just as good. Meantime the world acclaimed him a Shakespeare and a Cervantes in one, and the most surprising thing about him is that the reverberation of the years of praise made absolutely no impression, not even a momentary impression, on his modesty. He let the people go wild with enthusiasm and was heartily glad of their cash. " They compare me with Shakespeare—not worthy to tie his shoe."

In his own day the topic oftenest discussed by intelligent people was the authorship of the Waverley Novels—who wrote them, one man or a dozen, Erskine, Tom Scott, Jeffrey, Walter Scott, or a combination of these and others. It grew to be an infliction at dinners and parties, because everybody had an opinion, and quidnuncs and cranks had the time of their lives. Bacon and Shakespeare was nothing to it. It does seem strange that a successful novelist should deny his authorship, but the persistent denial can be explained.

At the age of twenty-five he published his first book of verse, translations from Bürger. Possibly because he was sure that his father, then alive, was right in saying that to be known as a poet among the canny solicitors who distributed business would hurt the young advocate in his profession, he withheld his name from the volume. It is interesting, too, to note that he employed Will Erskine to negotiate the whole affair with the publishers. On this early occasion as ever afterwards there was this anomalous reserve in Scott, anomalous because no man had a keener eye for business than he, and none so solidly laid down all the items to be discussed and concluded as he ; nobody so quick to point out wherein his missionaries had allowed the other side to assume too much.

Accordingly he began his literary career with an anonymous volume ; and his sheriffdom, his legacies, his Clerkship of Session and other successes made him independent of solicitors. He published his own substantial poems under his own name, but he edited Swift, who had hardly ever owned one of his books, though so many had been successful ; and his own old friend Henry Mackenzie was as fond of concealing his authorship. The notion of anonymity became familiar to him, appealed to him, became his preference. . . .

Because he considered himself something much better than a literary man. In his mind a *gentleman*, a man with an estate and with or without a title, was much superior in the scheme of things to any literary man whomsoever. The things of the mind were casual and rather inferior. The acres, the political power and wealth were the thing.

He had good use for the money that the writing of books brought in, but to be a recognised literary man, on the level of Wordsworth and a hundred others, was distasteful to him. He was a Scottish gentleman ; if he had a gift for producing popular books it was all very good business, but the serious affairs of life were not to be dragged down in the comparison. For, having that feeling, he ventured to argue the point. Literature is created by interested people for the amusement of the idle, a tumbling on the stage for gain. Let us rouge our faces and paint our eyebrows so that off the stage it shall not be known that gentlemen abase themselves in such a way.

Meantime we buy acres with the proceeds, put up a château and entertain like a monarch.

In this astonishing world there is nothing so perplexing as the judgments of men.   And the judgments of men on Sir Walter's novels, poems, and editions become not only strange but fatiguing.   The solemn descriptions of the stories, the disquisitions on his metres—those broken-winded metres— the silliness of the reviewers who did not realise the perfections of the poems, and finally the excruciating excerpts. . . .

Few things are quite so pathetic as the hacking of verse that resounds in chapter xxv. of the *Life of Scott*.   When he had written his verses on " The Field of Waterloo," John and James Ballantyne both offered some verbal alterations, and Sir Walter's replies to their criticisms are in this vein :

" Fair Brussels, thou are far behind," wrote Scott.   " I don't like this line," said James.   " Stet," replied Scott.

I read his significant comments on his own productions many times over before I realised that his modesty on the subject of his books was absolutely sincere.   He had no belief in their merits.   No man on earth except himself could have endured so much praise and have refrained from believing himself a classic.   But there was in Scott a stark strength that resisted all impression.   No man of his time or since, however critical of Scott's literary achievements he may have been, could say anything about them that the Sheriff has not implied or said before him.   Listen to Scott on the subject of Scott :

" I pique myself more on my compositions for manure than on any other compositions whatsoever "—Shakespeare's or Scott's or anybody's else.   And in 1822—" I was never fond of my own poetry, and am now much out of conceit with it." In fact, he had to do the writing business, and when finished with it he was heartily glad to hear no more about it.   " Praise gives me no pleasure and censure annoys me."

These quotations and opinions signify reality in regard to Scott, and should be pondered carefully.   It is by the apprehension of such sincerities that he is to be understood.

He seldom knew when he had done a good thing, but neither did his advisers, witness Erskine and Ballantyne on

Waverley. He thought Mrs. Cockburn's imitation of "The Flowers of the Forest" a real Border ballad, though before his time Burns had detected that it was a thing "of yesterday." He thought the frightful doggerel of "Hardyknute" "a noble imitation of the best style of old ballad," and when he recited it to Byron the noble poet was so agitated that others present asked Scott what he had been saying to upset Byron. This is the kind of thing it is :

> "To horse, to horse, my royal liege !
>   Your foes stand on the strand.
> Full twenty thousand glittering spears
>   The King of Norse commands.
>
> .   .   .   .   .   .
>
> With smileless look and visage wan
>   The wounded Knight replied :
> ' Kind chieftain, your intent pursue
>   For here I maun abide.'
>
> .   .   .   .   .   .
>
> Cease, Emma, cease to hope in vain :
>   Thy lord lies in the clay.
> The valiant Scots nae rievers thole
>   To carry life away."

Time and again immediately after writing verse or prose he was doubtful whether it was good or bad. When he wrote "Bonnie Dundee," as good a singing song as one could desire, he wrote down his doubts about it in his journal. And even in the matter of titles he who had an exquisite faculty for devising appropriate names sometimes did himself no justice. His publishers changed some of his titles, and at least in one case Constable bettered the master. Scott was busy on a volume that he proposed to call " Letters on the History of Scotland, addressed to a Family of Young Persons," and Constable suggested the title of *Tales of a Grandfather*.

The Ballantynes, on the other hand, were sometimes very careless. They corrected Scott's rapid poetry with solemnity. He depended on them, both on James and John, to keep him right in details ; for while another author would draft, correct, lay aside in order to re-read and finish, Scott dashed off his MS, sent it to the printers, and hated to look at it again. And the Ballantynes who scrutinised his chapters let pass the most outrageous blunders.

In *Old Mortality* a band of soldiers sets out to capture Burley, who has left in company with Henry Morton; but they vanish into air, while Burley spends the night at Morton's. In chapter viii. Scott states that "the soldiers had already bound and secured their prisoner," Henry Morton. When Mause Headrigg's harangue is finished and the soldiers move away, it is surprising that "they did not bind their prisoner."

He depended on his auxiliaries to see that such things were corrected, and too often the auxiliaries failed him.

It is just because there was in Scott no spiritual impulse that the main themes of his novels and poems are never successful as artistic efforts. His heroes have no life; their pursuits have no reality nor worth. His heroines are beautiful and strike attitudes, talk interminably in the oratorical way of heroines, and are ineffectual. But one of the strongest characteristics of Scott was his interest in criminals: he liked the bare stern life of the peasant, admired and cherished in memory their downright phrases, doted on the exploits of old freebooters, and had a passion for antiquity. Accordingly his minor characters, almost always a success, reflect the more sincere parts of his own character, deep and sympathetic as it was.

Time and again, referring to his lack of success with his nominal heroes, he lamented that the scoundrel of the book always ended up as the hero. The only occasion on which the "heroes" show any animation is when they are enraged, and then in the flowing torrent of their indignation there does appear some light, some reflection of lifelikeness.

Like most men, he was sometimes disgusted with the apparatus of his daily toil, and on Hogmanay 1808, when no doubt all the rest were enjoying themselves, he expressed in a letter his "great abhorrence of pen and ink." He was recommending a friend to get hold of some new book or other and do a good hacking review of it for the new *Quarterly*. He specially mentioned Macneill, a poet who had a quarto on the market, and who is remembered by the devotees of Scottish song as the author of "Jeanie's Black Ee," the frightful transcript with a frightful tune of the exquisite "Lison Dormait," which has as exquisite a melody.

It was when he was forty-three, and tired of writing verse, that he was astonished to discover that a novel written in six weeks brought in more money than two years spent with excitement and puzzling of brains over a long poem. It is difficult to understand why Scott took so long over his poems. His rhymes were very vague, and his forms of verse were invariably of the loosest and easiest kind. But even with easy verse he had to concentrate himself, and could not do as he did with prose. When writing novels or other prose he wrote whenever he was at rest, even with his family talking by his side. When travelling, staying at inns or private houses, he rarely started in the morning without sending off or leaving a packet for the printer. The writing was done as an extra, the last thing at night or first thing in the morning. And though he was a terrific worker, he was the kind of man that does five different tasks at a time better than one, and who works the better and harder if interrupted now and then. Interruptions are refreshment and relief to this type of man.

Lockhart, writing about 1837, remarked that it would always be considered one of the most pleasing peculiarities in Scott's history that he was the friend of *every* great contemporary poet. When we realise that he had no acquaintance with Landor, Coleridge, Shelley or Keats, who were all at their best during his time, this seems strange ; but it did not seem strange to Lockhart. These four names to Lockhart and Scott, and to most of their generation, signified nothing worth mentioning. Mr. Gifford, in Scott's opinion, was " a manly English poet, very different from most of our modern versifiers," an opinion with which, in so far as it may refer to these four great names, we can heartily agree. Scott knew and respected Wordsworth. He also knew Byron, Moore, Crabbe, Hogg, and "that true genius," as Lockhart called him, William Howison of Clydegrove.

When he was nearly fifty, Scott wrote " I have no habits of friendship and scarce those of acquaintance with Coleridge. I have not even read his autobiography " ; and at another time when writing to one Reverend Mr. Maturin, a successful author of the time who had written a nasty article about Coleridge as a preface to one of the reverend gentleman's popular novels, he said :

" Let me entreat you to view Coleridge's violence as a thing to be contemned, not retaliated. The opinion of a British public may surely be set in honest opposition to that of one disappointed and wayward man. You should also consider as a good Christian that Coleridge has had some room to be spited at the world, and you are, I trust, to continue to be a favourite with the public."

This is queer reading. But there were only two great names in English literature in the days of Scott, and these were Byron and himself. They impressed not only their countrymen, but the readers of books abroad. Scott was mobbed by the adoring Parisian crowds, and Byron's melancholies were the joy of Germany, while Keats's volume was described by a disillusioned purchaser as a take-in, and Leigh Hunt did not consider the verses it contained good enough for his magazine.

Scott greatly respected Wordsworth, his poems and his judgments, but Wordsworth's criticism of his books was straight from the shoulder. He had what is called a masculine way with him, and it says a good deal for the more masculine Scott that he took no offence at Wordsworth's acknowledgment of the present of a volume and his contempt of Scott's labours.

" Thank you for *Marmion*. I think your end has been attained. That it is not the end which I should wish you to propose to yourself you will be well aware. . . ."

It was in September 1803, when Scott was thirty-two and Wordsworth was thirty-three, that they were introduced by a common acquaintance, one Stoddart.

There is a touching characteristic about their first meeting. Wordsworth and his sister left their carriage at Roslin, walked down the two miles of Roslin glen to Lasswade, and arrived at Scott's cottage before Walter and his wife were up. This was before Sir Walter began his early rising.

Scott and Wordsworth charmed each other ; the Wordsworths walked on and Scott joined them in a couple of days at Melrose. He saw them again at Jedburgh, and pleaded with them not to come into court, where they would see him cut a strange figure ; but they did casually see him in cocked hat and sword, marching in the Judge's procession to the sound of one cracked trumpet.

Wordsworth was surprised and pleased at the deference paid to any mention of the young Sheriff's name. At the Melrose inn it was provisionally arranged that Scott and he should sleep in the same room, but the landlady told him bluntly that she could not settle it till she was sure that the Sheriff had no objection.

They walked together southward for another day or two.

"Wherever we went with him," said Wordsworth, "he seemed to know everybody and everybody seemed to know and like him."

The impression he gave Wordsworth was that he attached less importance to literary reputation and the law than to his sports and social amusements. No doubt this was a correct impression, though it is not to be forgotten that all the novels and most of his verse were unborn.

Wordsworth had three different attitudes towards those he met. In his verse he praised them wholeheartedly ; to their faces he gave them frank critical opinions, and privately or after they were dead he described them with truth and with merciless force. On Scott he made this profound observation :

"As a poet Scott cannot live, for he has never in verse written anything addressed to the immortal part of man."

Like Landor, Sir Walter had a good esteem of Southey, wrote to him that he had read "Madoc" four times—is there one man on earth now who has read "Madoc" four times ?— and prophesied that it would in time take its place at the feet of Milton. "I am not such an ass as not to know that you (Southey) are my better in poetry."

He had a huge respect for Joanna Baillie, and his many long letters to her are the dullest he ever produced. Writing to her he assumed a matronly respectability that paralysed his faculties. He whose endings even were always bright and happy sank so low as to finish a letter to her :

" Believe me honoured in permission to subscribe myself your affectionate and unworthy brother in the Muse."

He considered her a greater poet than Wordsworth or Shelley or Coleridge or Keats or Southey or Landor or himself.

Mrs. Baillie, who was never married, solemnly announced to her friends when she was about fifty that she had taken over the appellation of Mrs., as Miss did not suit her advancing years. To her brother the doctor, Scott once dispatched by ship a hamper of game addressed " Dr. Baillie, London," because at the moment he did not know the exact address.

He once wrote that " in lyrical poetry Dryden must be allowed to have no equal." By the time he said so both Wordsworth and Coleridge had written their best : Burns had lived and died, and the songs of the nameless Elizabethans were in his hands.

But he was never so delighted with any book as with *Pepys's Diary*. In Pepys he found the qualities he loved, strength, expressiveness, enjoyment of every hour, acute observation, a habit of prospering, and domestic scandal. The phrases of Pepys were often in his mouth, for it was easy to translate his own gusto into Pepysiana.

He saw himself as clearly as he visualised Pepys, and he discerned no nonsense about either. The literary idol of the time took the idolatry with a good-humoured divine smile, and laughed at it all when the worshippers went away. Every educated person in the kingdom talked about him every day or so, and he went his sincere, innocent way untouched, unconcerned, uplifted. He shrank with physical repugnance from praise, and enjoyed telling a story that exhibited himself as a disillusionment.

Once Charlotte and he went to the opera in London when all the stars in the musical world were on the stage and " all the great oneyers and burgomasters " were in the boxes. Scott and his wife were in the stalls. " The fiddlers and their abominations," as he called *entr'actes*, and the repetitions of singers signified less than the beat of a kettledrum to Scott, and his resource was at his hand. He slept when the curtain came down. While the fiddlers were at their abominations the cultivated audience as usual conversed in loud tones, and a young enthusiastic lady beside Mrs. Scott was naturally discussing the author of *Waverley*, as no doubt many more behind their fans were. Time and again she said :

" I would give the world to see Sir Walter Scott."

It grew at last too much for Charlotte, who had a sardonic vein that was dear to the Sheriff, and she looked at the young lady, caught her eye, impressively pointed to the stout, ugly, sleeping gentleman at her side, and nodded several times very significantly.

His portrait, idealised, vulgarised and softened, was yet too well known for the original to be mistaken. The lady got the shock of her life.

CHAPTER XVI

HIS SOCIAL AND POLITICAL VIEWS

To those who have a passion for reforming the world, orthodoxy
is the most puzzling characteristic of mankind. The greater
number of men and women do as their companions do and
think the thoughts of the unintelligent, but there is a higher
order of educated men, who have capacity enough to perceive
the emptiness of many things that are honoured and who yet
revere and defend all the paraphernalia that once assisted
the functions of essential life and are now outworn. They
still see all creation through the lewd rags that were once the
garment of holiness ; they look for inspiration to sources
that have passed from leadership to parasitism of the coldest
kind ; they put government to no question, for their fathers
have settled beforehand the opinions they are to detest. They
are for things as they exist and as they have existed. Point
out to them an injustice that affects ten million people and
they will persist in remedying the case of the individual. That
the common man should expect to be or imagine himself
worthy to live as they, is the end of the world. They perhaps
believe that success means merit, and that all whose ancestors
accumulated wealth are of superior nature. Yet landowners
have been known to be ignorant, cruel, pug-nosed even, while
a few horny-handed labourers may be found who have the
faces and hearts of Apollo and Hermes. . . .

Orthodoxy despises the vulgar and is itself vulgar. The
intangible aspirations of its generation it considers senseless,
ridiculous, wicked. It takes pleasure in the folly, the dis-
organisation, the crimes of the past, because they are sancti-
fied as romantic ; the pageant of power is beauty in its eyes,
not, as it almost invariably is, an oppression and a hindrance.
No historian who ever lived has dealt justly with any episode

of history.   The heroes of the nations are nearly all scoundrels ;
the traditions of the peoples are one long series of misguided
passions, while the call to raise up the spirit and the life of
mankind sounds in the ears of men continually and is in every
generation stifled and extinguished.

In this orthodox frame of mind Scott lived and died. His
fiercest angers were directed against those who had not and
desired votes, who seethed in the boiling oil of the growing
industrial frenzy, and who burned to extract from their
drudgery some joy of life and labour.   And if his soul flamed
with hatred of the spiritual impulse of his day, he had as
unworthy a contempt for the art of which he was a master,
though certainly he knew he was not such a master as he was
supposed to be.   The deeper one divines the attitude of Scott
to literature the less patience is possible with him.   He prized
the money that his books brought him a thousand times more
than the fame.   He would rather have been Duke of Buccleuch
or Duke of Blankshire than Shakespeare—a million times
rather.   It gave him pain to have his station in literature
compared with the greatness of a general of an army.   Literature was only a natural gift that might be found in peasants,
but a general had attained to the rank of a gentleman, was
always titled, and was in the forefront of recognition.   There
was no comparison between General Tufto and him.   He
subdued his intelligence gladly to the idea of the supremacy
of those whose merit it was to be born important : he could
gush for an hour about the ensuing calamity of a duke's death
to ten thousand people—as if another duke were not quite ready
to draw the rents and the dividends and to distribute a share in
charity and jobs, and as though the duke were a necessity to the
labourers instead of the labourers being a necessity to the duke.

It was this carelessness of the fame he had earned that
enabled him in Wordsworth's presence to quote Wordsworth
with gusto, while Wordsworth also quoted Wordsworth at
great length and nobody quoted Scott, and Lockhart boiled
with rage.   For Lockhart held literature in some estimation,
and Scott's serenity was due to the fact that he considered it
only a profitable amusement.   His spirit reposed on Abbotsford and on his acres.

He was the antithesis of the intellectual or idealist politician. His dream was of solid acres, castellated, well-planted, with a hundred and one pleasant paths of his own planning through woods every oak and larch of which had been planted with his own hands. He had no vision of the State as an organic thing tending towards strange new ways corresponding with discovery of power and development of material. He was certain that everything essential to his own peace of mind could be kept just as it was, if people would only be as reasonable as himself.

If he had had more social conscience he would have had less interest in his characteristic pursuits. He often referred to his craving for land, which was so strong that whenever he had a chance of buying any in the neighbourhood of Abbotsford he paid any price rather than let it escape him, and almost always bought it with borrowed money. This craving, however, has been too hastily reckoned as a mere bourgeois desire to rise in the world, to accumulate, and to prosper. It is granted that such ambitions were greatly in his mind, but in his mind was much more. He was peer of the best and greatest of those who have loved their native soil with the burning desire of communion and creation. He had imaginations of wonderful things that he could do with land that was his own, and he had the supreme satisfaction of clothing a bare countryside with beauty. There are very few who have even a remote notion how to create a landscape, though the stay-at-home squires of old time had both the gift and the goodwill, as the acres of England witness. Scott had this sublime passion, and his passion was filled full.

Listen to the poignancy of his regrets when in the crash of his dreams wild rumours of disaster were coming through, and gleams of hope tormented him :

" My heart clings to the place I have created—there is scarce a tree on it that does not owe its being to me. . . . Sad hearts, too, at Darnick, and in the cottages of Abbotsford. I have half resolved never to see the place again. How could I tread my hall with such a diminished crest ? . . . My dogs will wait for me in vain. It is foolish, but the thought of parting from these dumb creatures has moved me more than

any of the painful reflections I have set down . . . I feel my
dogs' feet on my knees—I hear them whining and seeking me
everywhere.

" I have walked my last on the domains I have planted—
sate the last time in the halls I have built. . . . I will not yield
without a fight for it. It is odd, when I set myself to work
doggedly, as Dr. Johnson would say, I am exactly the same
man as I ever was. . . ."

His politics ran parallel with his social views. " The constitution," meaning the king, the peerage and the laws as they
stood at the moment of any dispute, were perfect in nature,
though nobody had more cutting things to say about person-
ages than Scott had. He had no spiritual impulse whatsoever in regard to the state of society, and this would not
be imputed to him as blame if he had not been a politician
whose attitude to the State was entirely wrongheaded. His
view of politics was briefly that every scheme of national
organisation was a fraud on landowners ; that the growing
industrialism which provided the problems of his time should
stew in its juice ; that to give votes to tradesmen was the
end of " the Constitution," and therefore of the eternal
truths.

His benefactions were large and constant, but I at least
would have much more satisfaction in them had they been
allied to any inkling of himself as the fellow of the unfortunate throughout the kingdom. But his private charities were
his notion of righteousness and soothed his mind, were, in short,
his substitute for making up his mind about the nation's
troubles. Much more satisfactory if he had had some pity
for, some understanding of, the sorrows of the industrial life
that was fermenting in his day. Curious that he had neither
pity nor understanding ; not a grain. He pursued with real
malice the earliest trade unionists, made every effort to
destroy them, desired to root them out by killing them. This
is the exasperating limitation of the really good-natured. They
are incapable of perceiving what is clear to restless and anxious
minds, that the chief aspect in which modern States appear
is one of disease, long engrained but eradicable, and eradicable
to the advantage of all.

Even in his own day many of his acquaintances told him.

12

and many of his friends hinted, that his political opinions were insufficient for an intelligent man. Much, of course, has to be discounted from his argumentative opinions, for disputes were high : much has to be put to the account of mere party opposition, the wrangles of the hour and the inertia of soul that follows prosperity : much also to breaking health after 1826. It was clearly seen, too, by Carlyle, his contemporary, that he lived in a generation that had lost the beliefs of former days, had acquired none of its own, and was terrified at scepticism. Accordingly its god was good form. But discounting all those personal and public items, we who perceive from this distance the springs of his spirit and the sequence of his years see that the social impulses and actions of Walter Scott were vicious, altogether at enmity with the only righteousness of his age, the spirit of Shelley in literature, of the reforming party in politics, and of the earliest trade unionists who endured the horrors of industry in the early nineteenth century. The most energetic actions of his life were directed against these best and purest spirits and against the chief national movement of his time, that which had in it most consideration for the future well-being of the nation.

The governing characteristic of Scott's temperament was expressed briefly by himself : " I am unfortunately furnished with a set of tastes and appetites which would do honour to the income of a duke if I had it." His life, his habits, his letters, his journal and his biography emphasise his pride in money and in the things money can buy. He strove all his life for one thing, prosperity ; and nothing shows more clearly than his own words and actions how little desire he had for anything but the wealth and prosperity of himself and his intimates. His highest notion of personal interest in mankind was to job for his friends and to give charity to any others whom by accident he saw needing it.

Scott's readers in his own generation were the wealthy. Some of his poems were published at two guineas, and the price of the novels was usually about the same. So he owed no debt to the millions of common men. But when he had scoundrels to draw he found them, as a rule, in the upper classes. His peasants or poor people are almost invariably admirable characters.   And he found in life his own best and truest friend in the peasantry.

Yet when we come to his private opinion about the population of the country, we find quite another matter.   Then we hear of "the rascal and uninstructed populace," "a poor, effeminate and vicious," "the lazy dross of a metropolis," "those who look for anything better than ingratitude from the uneducated and unreflecting mass of a corrupted population must always be deceived "—this from a student of politics and about the common people of Scotland.   "The rogue Radicals " occupied an enormous part of his thoughts, and provided the people whom he was anxious to destroy.   His wife wondered why they were not all taken and hanged.   In 1830 Anne wrote that her father's conversation was "nothing but croaking about the evil times."   "How willing the vulgar are to gull themselves when they can find no one else to take the trouble."   When the Reform Bill passed for the first time Scott was no longer himself, and I forbear to descant on his outbursts about that time and on that subject.   Yet though there is no doubt that these were his views, there is an air of unreality, of opinions held without conviction, even of sycophancy, about his attitude towards the worldly great. Of the artistic great he had no opinion at all, but before dukes, kings and generals he abased himself.   He, before whom the world threw pearls, declared that the courtesies shown him by the Duke of Wellington after they were introduced in 1815 were the highest distinction of his life.   This is how he finished a letter to the duke in 1827 :

" I have too long detained you, my Lord Duke, from the many high occupations which have been redoubled upon your Grace's head, and beg your Grace to believe me, with an unusually deep sense of respect and obligation, my dear Lord Duke, your Grace's much honoured and grateful humble servant,

" WALTER SCOTT."

It is amazing to find Scott at fifty-five writing so.   The nauseating servility, the exaggeration of the trifling obligement, the humble excuse for inflicting on the Duke of Wellington a letter from mere Sir Walter Scott, the thick-skinned repetition of the titles, so different from Johnson's ironical use of them sixty or seventy years before, present an aspect of Sir Walter that is inexcusable, not to be defended for a moment by any notion that such grovelling was the custom of the time. It was not.

He followed the duke's career with the energy and enthusiasm of an ideal. He continually referred with awe and distant respect to the generals who led a few thousand men into battle. In his opinion those who had attended lectures on tactics—or had bought themselves on—were the supremest of men, far greater in grain than poets, painters, or musicians, even somewhat greater than landowners and lawyers.

In 1813 or 1814, when someone dug up the mutilated body of Charles I., a little of the hair found its way as a great favour to Scott. He accepted it as such, and turned some Indian mohurs into a massive gold ring in which the hair was set. The word REMEMBER was inscribed on it in highly-relieved black-letter, and for some years he wore this ring constantly, possibly till he realised in his own flesh what true sorrow was. But it is not to be forgotten that in his day the Court of Session took a holiday yearly on 31st January in memory of King Charles's death.

When a duchess of Buccleuch died he almost called in question the Eternal Wisdom that had so early summoned her from this wretched world, etc. etc. He had skipped the logic class at college, and, as I have said, there is something insincere about it all.

Scott was a lawyer before he was a successful author, and his instinct for the right way to get on in the legal profession was as keen as his instinct for the popular kind of thing in verse and prose. His father ought not to have worried himself about Walter's dilatory ways and small measure of success. Walter was born to be advanced by methods that are as successful to-day as they were a hundred years ago. But that success was at first so small that it might have worried any one. It did not worry Scott. His first year's income as an advocate was £24, 3s.; the second, £57, 15s.; the third, £84, 4s.; the fourth, £90; the fifth, £144, 10s. On £144, 10s. a year he married, and next year his income was £79, 17s.; the next year it was £135, 9s.;

then £129, 13s., £70, £202, 12s., and, at the age of thirty-one, £228, 18s. This average yearly income of £122, 10s. for eleven years was all Scott could make at the Bar. When his father died he got about £5000, and his uncle Robert's death provided him with as much or more ; but young Scott had other ways of getting on in the world.

He had early realised the value of " sound principles " as a means of advancement. His volunteering had led him into the company of the Earl of Dalkeith and Lord Montagu, brothers of the Duke of Buccleuch, and he had shown them great attention and respect. Two years afterwards they got the duke, who " owned the county," to approach Lord Melville, the Secretary for Scotland (as one may call him), for the vacant job of Sheriff of Selkirkshire. No doubt other hawks were after the quarry, so all the influence that could be got was brought to bear. Scott " always remembered with gratitude the strong intercession on this occasion of Lord Melville's nephews, Robert Dundas of Arniston, Lord Advocate, and the Right Honourable William Dundas." The Honourable Robert Dundas, son of Lord Melville, had been at school with him, and had been a volunteer with him, so he coaxed his father too. Lockhart proudly clinches these various qualifications of Scott for advancement with this final and unanswerable recommendation : " The duke and this able minister had both seen Scott frequently under their own roof and been pleased with his manners and conversation ; and he had by this time come to be on terms of affectionate intimacy with some of the younger members of either family." On such grounds Scott, who had never made £250 a year, was jobbed into a place of £300 a year. The posts of many Sheriffs-principal, now as then, were almost sinecures. Millions of pounds have been drawn in these posts throughout Scotland, and the lucky holders continue to practise at the Bar, or, like Scott, hold other jobs and draw large salaries for hearing half a dozen cases a year or less, and signing a few forms, the work in which is done by clerks.

Scott was so little required that for some years he lived in Edinburgh. Eventually he had to reside in his sheriffdom, but he kept his Edinburgh house and attended the Court of Session daily.

At thirty-five he saw a chance of getting a clerkship in the Court of Session. An old clerk was willing to retire, but wanted to draw the salary of £800 (it rose to £1300) a year, and as all he had to do was to totter to a chair and sit there for four hours a day (with a holiday on Mondays) while the clerk's clerk on a pound a week did the work for the clerk to sign, the old man could make his own terms. Scott agreed to do the work for nothing till the old man should die, and again he got the Duke (now *his* Duke, formerly Earl of Dalkeith) to job him on.

Thus his two permanent posts were jobs, got from his patrons at the expense of better and harder-working lawyers. In 1816–17 he tried to get the Duke of Buccleuch to job him into a third and best post, a Barony of the Exchequer. His Grace found himself unable to assist, as he was not at the moment in favour with the Cabinet, and so Scott's one qualification was exhausted. No doubt the person appointed was no more capable than he, but there is as little doubt that those who were most capable never stood any chance of the post.

In turn he was never happier than when his own personal influence got his relatives, friends and dependants into posts appropriate to them. The episode of his appointment of his brother Tom to a job is still doubtfully to his credit, for the charge against him though raised by Lord Holland in the Lords was never answered satisfactorily. The charge was that at the very moment when Walter Scott was acting as Secretary of a Commission (another job from which he expected but naturally did not get advancement) on the legal system of Scotland, he appointed his brother to a post, knowing that within a few months the office would be abolished and that compensation and a pension would have to be paid to any holder of it. Tom fled to the Isle of Man and Canada, never entered the office door, but annually drew the pension.

Scott's notion of society was patronage, the world's work carried on by the whim of the powerful. He got Lockhart some fairly remunerative literary work the day after he met him for the first time—and Lockhart was a relative of his neighbour Torwoodlee. He was soliciting a legal job for Lockhart at the moment when Murray offered the latter the editorship of the *Quarterly*. He regarded these favours as personal payment for reverence to dukes and other great men. " The whole burgher class of Scotland are gradually preparing for radical reform. . . . The gentry will abide longer by sound principles, for they are needy and desire advancement for their sons, and opportunities, and so on." The nakedness under the " principles " with which " the gentry " in all ages have clothed themselves is here well exposed, but what shall we say of the spirit of him who wrote such callous hypocrisy ?

He appears to have imagined that if the paltry electoral reform that the middle classes were striving for were carried, " Scotland, completely liberalised as she was in a fair way of being, would be the most dangerous neighbour to England."

Scott is at his very best, most humane, most sympathetic, generous and reasonable when talking or writing to his inferiors in station. His letters to the Duke of Buccleuch and to the various titled ladies with whom he was proud to correspond are often unworthy of him, and between him and those whose station corresponded with his own no generous thought on the subject of the nation or of the future was ever exchanged. And the ill-nature of Scott's attitude to the people is made plain by the fact that he imagined much more appalling wickedness on the part of the British upper classes in whom he desired for ever to concentrate all power, property and honour, than in the lower and middle classes whom he was determined to keep unenfranchised and ignorant. In 1809, when Perceval became Prime Minister, Scott prophesied that Bonaparte would " send a few hundred thousands among our coach-driving Noblesse and perhaps among our Princes of the Blood " —that the king's sons and the nobility would take Bonaparte's money to serve Bonaparte. And another time it gave him pain to observe that the king's brothers could not even behave decently, to say nothing of their public immoralities.

In communicating to Laidlaw his intention of raising a Border brigade and a personal quota of about sixty men to exterminate the Radicals, he wrote—" I beg of you, dear Willie, to communicate my wish to all who have received a good turn at my hand or may expect one." Another inducement was " when work is scarce we offer pay for them playing themselves." " They will perhaps have to fight with the pitmen and colliers of Northumberland for defence of their firesides." There is, of course, no doubt that the real intention of the Western weavers and of the Northumberland colliers was to destroy the firesides of the Scottish Border cottages, slay the agricultural labourers and their infants, violate their wives, and perform all the other atrocities with which our newspapers make us so familiar, whenever in any part of the world freedom stirs in the spirit of men ?   Indeed no.   This romantic poet was anxious to raise an army in order to kill off as many as possible of the miners and weavers who were so wicked as to form trade unions and agitate for more wages and for votes. By "defending their firesides," the athletic, armed agriculturists would make an end once for all of trade unions.   It is melancholy to record that as Government money was not forthcoming to defray the expenses of this brigade it was not raised.

Writing to Morritt of Rokeby in June 1810, when he was neither a youth nor an old man, he said, " It is disgraceful to see the legislature of this mighty kingdom, representatives of all the power, wisdom and property of Great Britain, insulted by the very scum of the earth, for such must the mob of Westminster be ; and very little better do I hold the factious demagogues of the Livery. . . ."

The dots are piquant ; perhaps Sir Walter even said damn. How pleasant is his indignation against the wealthy citizens of London who demonstrated against the representatives of *all* the property of this mighty kingdom !

Till November 1830 Scott was himself, though shaken. In that year every newspaper was full of reports of riots and burnings, much the same diversions as the ladies recently gave the public when they too desired votes.   But Scott, who had rejoiced in the festering smell, the bones and the bloodstained relics of the battlefield of Waterloo, was worried to death by the broken windows and the smoking haystacks of London and the provinces.   Earl Grey brought in a Reform Bill which to him signified revolution and the end of everything.   Even Laidlaw hailed it as the beginning of the millennium ; but Laidlaw was incapable of impressing Scott.   Ballantyne was going round to that way of thinking, and Scott was nasty to him.   Cadell had nothing but contempt for Toryism of the ancient keep-them-down kind, seeing clearly that there was more of a career in front of employers if the employed were decently educated, fed and housed; and Cadell was his publisher, the man whom on the whole he spoke to, wrote to, and dealt with most. But Cadell would not risk his bread and butter by talking politics to his author, so Scott " croaked about the evil times " to Anne.

While, in March 1831, he was grudging his best friends an hour of his company, because they kept him from the writing of books that meant to him the redemption of his honour, he gave four full days to the preparation of an address from " the County of Selkirkshire " against the Reform Bill—" certainly in my best style." Laidlaw the Whig, who welcomed the Reform Bill as the beginning of the millennium, told him it was the best thing he had ever written. Six county gentlemen—" the County of Selkirkshire "—met and adopted another address—" too milk-and-water to attract notice. . . . I was a fool to stir such a mess of skimmed milk." But nobody kicked Laidlaw. And several of the " County of Selkirkshire " had previously visited him for the express purpose of urging him to draw up a resolution with a sting in it.

On 18th May of the same year he went to the Roxburghshire general election at Jedburgh. There was no reason for his journey, as the result was a foregone conclusion, and his family tried to persuade him to stay at home. As usual with good-natured men, he agreed with everything they said, and let them sleep in peace, but at 7 a.m. his carriage was ordered and he was off. Lockhart went with him. The town was in an uproar. Sir Walter, who had and controlled many votes, and thought it a calamity that a weaver should have a vote, was pelted with stones. A few fell into the carriage, but none touched him. He put up his carriage at an inn near the Shortreeds' and walked to the booth between Lockhart and young Shortreed. He was greeted with boos and blasphemies; a woman spat on him from a window, but Lockhart thought that this escaped his notice. Inside the court he tried to speak from the Bench, but not a word was heard. For the County of Roxburgh young Harden was returned by what Lockhart calls " a great majority," forty to nineteen, and the streets rapidly grew dangerous. Scott was advised not to go back the way he came, and accepted the invitation of a Whig to go by byways to his house outside the town and to have his carriage sent thither.

The carriage was brought round by Peter, and Scott escaped. There was a shower of stones at the bridge at the foot of the town, and Lockhart indeed thought that an attack had been arranged there, but there were two troops of dragoons on the spot and their presence was sufficient to protect him. A phrase shouted at him preyed on his mind—" Burk Sir Walter."

A couple of months later, about Biggar, he saw from his carriage a carter maltreating his horse, and he cried to the man in great indignation. The carter cried as angrily to him. His heart bled for the sufferings of the horse, but the sufferings of his fellows, men, women, and children, in that disorganised industrial time merely increased his hatred of them.

And here it is necessary to go somewhat deeper into Scott's views on trade and the early trade unions, and into his practice in hunting out these victims. Factories and industrialism troubled him greatly ; he perceived neither their necessity, to which we of a later age have reconciled ourselves, nor any good in them, in masters, men or material. But it was to him red rank revolution that a band of miners or weavers should combine and lodge with the owner of a pit or a factory a notice for a shilling a day more. Of course he saw revolution in everything ; he had not a shred of political judgment.

Here are his views, at the age of forty-six, on the relief of the industrial poor :

" There would be no means so effectual as that of taxing the manufacturers according to the number of hands which they employ on an average, and applying the produce in maintaining the manufacturing poor. If it should be alleged that this would injure the manufacturers, I would boldly reply : ' And why not injure or rather limit speculations, the excessive stretch of which has been productive of so much damage to the country and to the population whom it has in so many respects degraded and demoralised ? ' "

He called a manufacturer who employed men a speculator

But the manufacturers made the nation's goods, paid wages, and created foreign trade. Not much speculation there. It is indeed speculation when a man buys land with bills founded on the credit of half a dozen different firms, and years or months in advance of his income. Such speculations ought to be limited. Nor is it to be forgotten that few shared so extensively and so securely in the profits of industry as the owners of the land on which railways, docks and factories were being built at the very time he spoke.

But, after all, a factory or pit owner had it in him to be a gentleman, even a landowner, and Scott was incapable of rancour against such men. Accordingly, he reserved most of it for the workmen, and he gave them full measure. Curious, by the way, to observe that the leisured public had in 1825 the same grievance against miners as they have nearly a hundred years later, namely, that if a miner can screw a living out of five days a week in the frightful pits, he is loth to go down six days a week. At a dinner party in 1825, Lord Melville and Scott and many more titled people groaned over this wicked and idle habit of the miners.

In 1819 he translated the self-reproach and terror of the governing class, helpless to organise industrialism or abate the sorrows of the homes of Britain, into the following phantasm— " The fearful thing is the secret and steady silence observed by the Radicals in all they do." But the episode in his life which I cannot forgive is even earlier, when he was forty-one, in the prime of health, success and adulation. In January 1812 he had begun to draw his £1300 a year as Clerk of Session, and his fame as a poet was world-wide. On 14th June of that year he wrote :

" Last week, learning that a meeting was to be held among the weavers of the large manufacturing village of Galashiels for the purpose of cutting a man's web from his loom, I apprehended the ringleaders and disconcerted the whole project ; but in the course of my enquiries, imagine my surprise at discovering a bundle of letters and printed manifestoes, from which it appeared that the Manchester Weavers' Committee corresponds with every manufacturing town in the south and west of Scotland and levies a subsidy of 2s. 6d. per man (an immense sum) for the ostensible purpose of petitioning Parliament for redress of grievances, but *doubtless*(!) to sustain them in their revolutionary movements."

That the weavers were meeting for the purpose of cutting a man's web from his loom and were advertising it to the countryside, I do not for an instant believe. It is as impudent a fabrication as the " doubtless to sustain them in their revolutionary movements."

Again on 4th August he referred to the matter as follows :

" There have been very serious disturbances among the manufacturers of the Midland counties which by the mistaken lenity of Government have been suffered to *assume an alarming degree of organisation. Correspondences have been carried on by the malcontents through every manufacturing town in England and Scotland, and the infection had even reached the little thriving community of Galashiels.* I was not long, however, of locating these associations and securing their papers : the principal rogue escaped me."

Altogether a pleasant picture of Walter Scott smashing up the earliest trade unions ! In his opinion the leader was a rogue, the movement was an infection, and it was a crime for the slaves of trade to join together to improve their wages and their conditions.

When the cry of " Burk Sir Walter " went up at Jedburgh on 18th May 1831 he was horrified. The cruelty of the phrase haunted him, though it is possible enough that the phrase was all the harm that was meant, and that there was no intention of laying a finger on him. But it was appalling that an important gentleman like himself should be threatened with violence while preaching to the people that they ought not to share the political advantages he possessed. As he brooded over this disgrace it is certain that he never once recalled the day in the year 1812 when he persecuted a more spiritual soul than his own, broke up a home, tore a man from his work and friends and sent him into exile. The world has confirmed the life-work and the point of view of that nameless agitator, and Scott's shameful callousness and active cruelty, demonstrated in his private correspondence where he had not the excuse of his official position, is not the least of those many defects of spirit that alienate the deeper regard of mankind from him.

I had written so far when I was astounded to find from his diary that this prosperous gentleman with the long memory had gone home from Jedburgh and had written this :

" The time at which I settled at Abbotsford, Whitsunday, 1811 " (it was 1812), " I broke up a conspiracy of the weavers.'

Astonishing callousness ! He had hunted to the hills a nobler spirit, a better man, than himself, and in the moment when the labours of the hunted prophet had been crowned with local success it never entered the heart of King Ahab to imagine that he had perhaps been, if not evil, at least mistaken.

Scott lived in a generation that had very little religious aim and less religious belief. The French Revolution and the long wars occasioned by the interference of other nations in the internal affairs of France had diverted men's minds from spiritual things. Keen enough to invoke the name of God in their quarrels, they had no place for Him in their hearts. The ancient orthodoxies were everywhere being questioned, and while sarcasms and intellectual squibs were permitted, any honest question about the serpent or about the bears that devoured the forty children who annoyed Elisha was treated as evidence of adultery, forgery and wife-beating.

As regards form of religion, Scott was bred a Presbyterian and apparently was ordained an elder in the Church. But his instinct was to follow in the track of the peerage of Scotland, which is nearly all Episcopal. At Ashestiel he never went to church, and while in winter he may have made casual appearances at a Presbyterian church, he read the English Church service in the country on summer Sundays. In later life he seems to have attended an Episcopalian chapel in Edinburgh and to have avoided the Established Church. It was the famous Dean Ramsay, an Episcopalian clergyman, whom he asked to conduct Charlotte's funeral service at Abbotsford. But in religion as in every other matter it is difficult to get to any depth in Scott. His deepest conjectures on the subject are about " rewards and punishments."

After Corunna he wrote to Southey, " We can only fight like mastiffs, boldly, blindly and faithfully. I am almost driven to the pass of the Covenanters when they told the Almighty in their prayers He should no longer be their God ; and I really believe a few Gazettes more will make me turn Turk or infidel."

The first sentence is pure British ; the second is no less so, but is lamentable. Nor is it altogether a joke ; it is an outburst of rebellion and despair ; but joke or no joke, the essential point is the assumption that God is a bestower of good things on Scott and Scott's friends and countrymen, and a with- holder of these good things from those others of mankind who quarrel with Scott. After this interpretation of the Creator, a person who ought to favour Scott, who is indeed rather more powerful than a Prime Minister or a general, and rather less reliable, it is unnecessary to inquire further into Scott's religion.

Those whom news of war has rendered sick at heart, till hope became almost an outrage on the intelligence, can sym- pathise with him. In 1809 he said he never suffered so much in his whole life from the disorder of spirits occasioned by bad news—he called it "affecting intelligence."

But while this kind of consideration was religion enough for him, while he himself had no particular belief in anything except prosperity and position, he had intense pleasure in any- thing that smacked of beliefs outworn. He loved to believe that people once intensely and passionately believed—in ghosts, in God, in toadstones, amulets, masses, kings. Even when writing in his own person he reflects this desire to believe. Describing the coronation of George IV., he found it " impos- sible to conceive a ceremony more august and imposing, and more calculated to make the deepest impression both on the eye and on the feelings. . . . The altar surrounded by the Fathers of the Church, the King encircled by the Nobility of the land and the Councillors of his Throne. . . ." And again he dilates on the moral grandeur of George IV.'s visit to Edin- burgh in 1822. " In fact, in moral grandeur it surpassed any- thing I ever saw."

How much of his content with the world just as it worked was due to the good fortune that was his all his boyhood, youth and maturity ? Success and goodwill were greatly re- sponsible for keeping him in tune with his world. If he had been for long years unsuccessful, poor and embittered, as with his natural gifts was very possible, the world would have seen another Walter Scott. " The feeling was born with me not to brook a disparaging look from an emperor," he writes, and rather feebly adds, " when I had the least means of requiting it in kind," meaning apparently that if he were to be the worse of requiting it he would refrain.

Into the details of his political and moral judgments it is not necessary to go much further ; they were lamentably deficient. He was the solid kind of man whose opinion commands great attention in his own country, whose politics, religion and morals are the sum-total of a few careful prejudices acquired before the age of fifteen, whose caution is accepted as more reliable than the reasoning of idealists, who indeed is an epitome of mankind as it exists, and who is therefore a good illustration of why mankind remains what it is. But I may instance a few of his judgments. In 1817 he did not believe that Canada would remain very long separated from the United States. He called the disastrous and ignorant George III. " the best of kings." He thought that the Bourbons would endure, though all the Whigs thought otherwise. His opinion after the war with America in 1814 was that Britain had given America encouragement to resume the war on a more favourable opportunity, and that it was Britain's business to have given the Americans a fearful memento that the babe unborn should have remembered. What unexpected blood-thirst is here ! And how wise were they who made that peace compared with Scott !

CHAPTER XVII

THE DISASTER OF 1826

NONE of the many writers about Scott has spoken of his money troubles with a grip of the subject. It was naturally very distasteful to Lockhart, Scott's son-in-law, and in his *Life of Scott* he not only refrained from going into it in detail, but was at times unjust, as when he spoke of Constable at the last moment flinging the counter-bills into the banks for what trifles they would fetch, and so piling up a debt of tens of thousands for no gain. Such a presentation of that fundamental matter shows that he did not investigate the causes of the financial disaster. He wrote about it in detached paragraphs, put most important items into mere footnotes, and altogether was reluctant to dwell on it, but laid the scourge of his sarcasm on both the Ballantynes. Them he exhibited in most ludicrous aspects, and conveyed the impression that John was a scoundrel, that James neglected his business, and that both were ridiculous creatures. And it must be said that it is difficult to resist that impression.

After the publication of the *Life* the Trustees of the Ballantynes published a volume in reply, making confusion worse confounded. Lockhart in answer wrote a pamphlet called "The Ballantyne Humbug Handled." It is almost impossible for any man to extract clear arguments and definite conclusions from these controversies; but happily the business habits of the time may be studied elsewhere, and the broad facts of the crisis, its causes and details, can be unravelled with patience. Scott himself could have written down an explanation of the whole thing on a sheet of paper.

The sum of the whole matter is that Sir Walter's habit of raising money for the purchase of land, and an iniquitous system of banking, brought about the crash. In the publishing business of those days every man with a shop seems to have set up as a banker with unlimited funds somewhere behind him. Instead of paying his author £2000 at a time for a copyright (for those were days when writing books was a profitable occupation) he gave the writer a promise to pay at six or twelve months, and got another publishing firm to add its security to his. The happy author went to the real bank and cashed the bill, but as often as not when the publisher was called on by the bank to pay the bill he had no cash to pay with. What did he do? He got the other publishing firm to give a bill at twelve months; he backed it and handed it to the bank, which, with that additional security, gave him another six or twelve months or more in which to pay. It is possible that the bank, being in possession of bills from each of the firms as principal debtor for the same sum, would make no trouble about future renewals.

The dangers attending a course of this kind were appalling, and James Ballantyne in 1814, twelve years before the crash, experienced the dire results of just such a mad makeshift. But Scott was as clear on the dangers of the system as any man. He knew, he realised perfectly the moment he was told of the insecurity of Hurst & Robinson, that his own bills, connected as they were with Constable who stood or fell with Hurst & Robinson, were likely to pull him down. There is little doubt that he heard of the following case from Constable, for it was as usual to that generous friend that Ballantyne appealed for a loan, and Scott may have laughed heartily over the way in which James was let in for a double payment. Though ready enough to assist, Constable was not the man to let such a good joke slumber, especially as he was not asked to be secret about it, and Sir Walter enjoyed the grim touch in a joke better than any other touch whatever.

In 1814, then, James bought wine for £75 from an ironmonger who needed money. With absolutely no foresight of danger he gave the ironmonger a bill for £75 at three months. The three months passed, Ballantyne had no money, and when the bank asked him to pay he took the daft step of going to the ironmonger (who had to empty his house to raise money) and getting him to give a bill at three months for the same amount. Ballantyne backed this bill and sent it to the bank so that it should stave off payment for other three months or more if necessary.

The second three months passed, the ironmonger went bankrupt, his creditors seized *both* bills and called on James Ballantyne, whose name appeared on both, to pay them £150, twice the price of his wine. And it had to be paid.

This is exactly the course and the cause of Scott's financial disasters. By raising money in this fashion in order to buy land he gave repeated hostages for one security, and was at length involved in the ruin of others, whereas if he had merely had to pay his own real debts the effort would not have disturbed him. He meant to pay them.

Constable was an Edinburgh publisher, but most of his books were distributed by Messrs. Hurst & Robinson, publishers in London, and the continual method of payment between them was by granting bills at three, six or twelve months, or even at two years. But it was quite a common thing for other London publishers to ask Constable to back their bills and for him to return the compliment, and as long as each believed the other firm solvent it was a mere act of courtesy. The frightful responsibility of the vast number of such bills in circulation gave them small concern, for the publishing businesses of the country were expanding in barometric response to expanding trade ; and even though Constable, for instance, may have had in circulation a mass of bills that he could not at a given moment meet by realising every asset he had in the world, he was confident of his security. His schemes of publishing were broad-minded and long of coming to full fruition, but his yearly profits were growing, and as long as the banks trusted him these banks for their own sake would refrain from calling in their bills, with all the disastrous consequences that such a course would entail.

There was much exchange of bills between Constable & Co. and Ballantyne & Co. There were four grounds for the creation of these bills : first, large payments to Scott for novels and poems ; second, the convenience of either business ; third, sums raised by Scott to buy land ; fourth, and as bad as all the rest put together, the counter-bills deposited with the banks to serve the purpose of postponing payment, and representing no asset on earth.

In August 1823, two and a half years before the crash, Constable wrote thrice to Scott pointing out that there were " bills current between Mr. Ballantyne's and Mr. Constable's firm without value," amounting to over £27,000, and pleading that the amount should be reduced to say £8000. The sum of £27,000 was raised by Scott as Ballantyne & Co. with Constable's backing ; and without a shadow of doubt, when Scott was unable to pay these sums as they fell due he requested Constable & Co. to manufacture bills for deposit with the banks. Therefore Scott, at his own option, was risking the chance of having to pay Constable's debtors, if Constable went bankrupt, the sum of £27,000 odd, besides the £27,000 he himself owed the banks. There is no escape from these plain facts, and nobody understood them so well as Scott himself. He calmly put Constable's suggestion aside, and left the floating bills at as large a figure as before.

Constable, of course, did not hesitate to use Ballantyne & Co. as they used him. He backed their bills and they backed his.

It is significant of Scott's hunger for land and of Constable's recklessness in raising money, that in 1821, before *The Fortunes of Nigel* was published, Scott had received from him the payment (in bills) for *four* other works of fiction, the very names of which he had not imagined.

It was perhaps impossible for the system of bill-accommodation to cease without some great disaster to warn everybody concerned, but things might have gone right enough for Scott if the London publishers with whom he was thus indirectly connected had not been half-witted. It was so easy to raise money by the system of bills, and bookselling was so slow, that one after another of the London publishers had raised money in that manner and had speculated it in all sorts of new industrial and trading ventures. By 1825 the clique of publishers had risked more money than they possessed, raised on each other's security from the banks, in South American mining shares, in railway and gas companies, and in other directions. Messrs. Hurst & Robinson, Constable's agents, had put £100,000 into such an astonishing venture as hops, and they had no end of commitments in the way of accommodations, and possibly in other trade schemes.

The banks pursued a course that was afterwards to incur the censure of the whole nation. They lent money right and left without proper limits or investigation, but their security was always doubled, and their claims had precedence over all other creditors. They were fairly safe with their multiplied securities, and they were ready even for a crash. But Scott was not prepared. He had entailed Abbotsford on his elder son, reserving the right to raise £10,000 on it; his library and household goods, which he would never have thought of realising except in dire necessity, were worth roughly another £10,000; the house at 39 Castle Street and its contents were worth say £4000, and he appears to have had no other assets except his share in the printing firm. His health, too, was already impaired; the frightful cramps of 1818 and 1819 had broken his great strength, and he had had slight premonitions of apoplexy.

In 1825 Scott was busy writing the *Life of Napoleon*, and it was the first time that a literary task exhausted him. It was, however, a great undertaking. He had to read huge files of English and French newspapers, extending over thirty years; he had to take notes and to assimilate the notes taken by amanuenses at his direction; he had to pore over maps, and puzzle out the course of battles; he had to interpret events that were by no means so simple as they appear now—and some of them are not clear yet, in spite of the commentation of a hundred years. Further, in spite of the symptoms of apoplexy he was eating and drinking in his usual hearty fashion. He was bulky, overfed, full of blood, and his lameness had increased so much that he had given up his habits of exercise. Accordingly he was in no condition to meet the trial of his full strength that confronted him at the end of that year.

When Lockhart got news from London that Constable's banker " had thrown up his book," he hurried across from Chiefswood to Abbotsford and found Sir Walter alone, having a cigar with whisky and water. Sir Walter treated the news with contempt, and Lockhart was greatly relieved; but next morning as he rose he was astonished to see Peter Mathieson with the carriage at his door. He saw Sir Walter rubbing his eyes, clearly new-wakened from sleep. He had been really concerned at the news, and had driven from Abbotsford to Constable's house at Polton and back during the night, a distance of nearly sixty miles altogether. Constable assured him that the story was false, but it was an omen of what was to come.

The news from London grew darker daily, and at a meeting between Scott, Constable, Cadell and Ballantyne, Constable convinced Scott that they would all do well to support Hurst & Robinson, whose bills the London banks were calling in. Constable sent them £5000, and proposed that Scott and he should borrow more for their assistance.

As one bank after another withdrew support from Hurst & Robinson they sent out frantic appeals to their business connections for assistance. One member of the firm had an estate somewhere, but even all his resources failed to fill the great void, and the appeals grew fast and furious. On 3rd January 1826, Scott, urged on by Constable and Cadell, raised £10,000 on the security of Abbotsford. His reservation of power to do this had been made with the intention of providing for his other children, but in this fashion their portion went into the whirlpool.

Meantime Constable, ill with dropsy and gout, had roused himself to journey to London, and was half-mad with excitement there. He sent for Lockhart and asked him to go straight to the Bank of England and support him, as a confidential friend of the author of *Waverley*, in an application for a loan of £100,000 to £200,000 on the security of all Constable's copyrights. Lockhart utterly refused, and in a few days Constable asked him to back an application to Sir Walter to borrow other £20,000 and transmit it to him in London. Lockhart could only reply that he would consult Sir Walter.

All concerned thought that if things just got steadier they would weather the storm ; and this might easily enough have been true of Constable and Scott. But the creditors of Hurst & Robinson's £100,000 and other speculations were hungry on the track, and the system of duplicate bills gave them the power to make men as unconnected with them as Scott and

Ballantyne pay twice over or even three times over in order to satisfy their claims.

How unable Scott was to endure the worry and uncertainty of that black winter is demonstrated by the fact that on 5th January 1826, after walking about Abbotsford all forenoon, he sat down at his desk and found to his horror that he could neither write nor spell, but put down one word for another— another premonition of apoplexy. But nothing was to be spared to him. On 16th January, in spite of his sacrifice of £10,000, he got the news of the failure of Hurst & Robinson. With their destruction the solvency of Constable & Co. was destroyed, for the creditors of Hurst & Robinson were entitled to call on Constable for payment of every penny of the bills on which the names of both firms appeared. With the fall of Constable & Co. fell James Ballantyne & Co., for the creditors of Constable were entitled to call on the partners to pay every penny of the bills on which the names of both these firms appeared—that is, at least double the sums really concerned.

When the whole tangle was unravelled the debts of Hurst & Robinson were put at about £300,000 ; Constable's were put at £256,000, and James Ballantyne & Co.'s at £117,000. Constable paid a dividend of 2s. 9d. in the pound, and Hurst & Robinson paid about 1s. 3d. The firm of James Ballantyne & Co., which was Walter Scott, paid twenty shillings in the pound, as all the world knows.

One can only say that, if he had been in Sir Walter's shoes, he would not have done it. Owing to a disorganised system of exchange, established with the sanction of Government and carried on without thought of the injury it caused to unoffending people, he was called on to pay at least twice, possibly three or four times, what he owed. He was actually made responsible for part of the debts of Hurst & Robinson, who were not connected with him in any way. No blame could have attached to him had he applied for a sequestration, but it would possibly have meant disentailing Abbotsford, and leaving it : it would have meant that he could be pointed to as a bankrupt who had not paid his debts to other people—though three-quarters of them were not his debts. Walter Scott's pride may have been narrow and fixed on worldly affairs, but no man ever lived whose pride was stronger than his. The law adjudged him liable for the sum? He would pay it or wear out his body in the trial.

Lockhart declared that the books of James Ballantyne & Co. were never balanced in the years before 1826. In 1822 at any rate, before or after James was received back as a partner, the books were audited. In that year the bills current against the firm, for Sir Walter's private accommodation, amounted to £26,896, 5s. 11d. and there were no bills on behalf of the firm for business purposes. It is said that this sum was increased by £8085, 3s. 1d. at the time of the disaster for discounts, stamps, and bank exchange, and by additional promissory notes for £17,142, 18s. 10d.; but I cannot find sufficient evidence of these last two sums. The whole current business debts due by the firm in 1826 were under £1000, and James Ballantyne's personal debts were under £100.

Constable's debts to the extent of £36,500 and some debts of Hurst & Robinson to the extent of £5500 had to be paid by Scott.

The following figures are merely an assumption of the manner in which Scott's debts were calculated, and it is to be remembered that I have not examined the books, if they exist anywhere, but the figures I give do approximate closely to Sir Walter's liabilities, and it is possible that they approach the facts of the case.

Supposing he had to pay his own personal liabilities twice over—

These were	{£26,896	5	11
	{ 26,896	5	11
Add the sum given as discounts, etc . .	8,085	3	1
Add the promissory notes given between 1822 and 1826	17,142	18	10
Add the bills of Constable on which the security of James Ballantyne & Co. appeared .	36,500	0	0
Add do. of Hurst & Robinson . .	5,500	0	0
	£121,020	13	9

Deduct actual price of house at 39 Castle Street . . .	£2,300			
Deduct actual price of furniture at 39 Castle Street, say . .	1,700			
		4,000	0	0
		£117,020	13	9

The details of the sum of £8085 for discounts, etc., and the particulars of the promissory notes amounting to £17,143 are obscure, but Scott put the signature of his firm to the bills for the purpose of lodging them in the bank and knew his responsibility for them. One other asset Scott had in his share of the printing business, but it was probably included in some of the above bills.

After examining these details I find it impossible to blame either Ballantyne or Constable for Scott's financial ill-luck. Neither could any man blame Scott. And he himself would have blamed anybody rather than the system which was responsible, for all the world knows his pathetic adherence to " the Constitution," by which he meant just things as they were in his day, even though they permitted such injustices to accumulate on his own head. When as a result of the unworthy manœuvres of the banks the Government proposed to curtail their powers, Scott published anonymous pamphlets against the proposals and fairly beat them with his own hand.

It is to be remembered that the frightful extent of his responsibilities did not dawn on Sir Walter late and suddenly. From the first moment of doubt in regard to the solvency of Hurst & Robinson he foresaw a great disaster, though he hoped to avert it. The point to emphasise, however, is that he realised immediately what he was in for, though possibly not to the exact extent of the £117,000 that were ultimately allocated to him as his debt.

He never forgave Constable for advising him to raise the £10,000 on Abbotsford only to throw it away. He never forgave him for the further urgencies of his appeals, when both knew that all chance of safety was gone; and certainly in this matter Constable acted in a dastardly fashion, explained to some extent though not excused by ill-health, frantic excitement and outraged pride. Scott broke with Constable once for all, and took the other partner, Cadell, as his publisher. It is curious to see how Lockhart, whose heart bled for Scott, cannot bring himself to lay nearly as much blame on Constable as Scott did. Lockhart beholds the long series of years in which the Ballantynes made rather a muddle of Scott's great successes, and concludes that if a man like Constable had had charge of them he would have created none of the mess that was made. But it is to be remembered that Scott was the managing director of the Ballantyne firms, and it is to be remembered, too, that after the crash he behaved to James with exactly the same kindness as before, employed him, associated with him, assisted him and esteemed him without bating a jot of trust.

It gives food for thought, too, that though he was journalising from day to day at this time and for years afterwards, he never once seems to have written down a detailed statement of the liabilities that he was called on to redeem. I am certain that he studied and knew them to the last detail.

On Constable he let loose a great deal of wrath which the publisher or his trustees certainly provoked. Scott had been paid by Constable's bills, which were entirely worthless, for the *Life of Napoleon* and for *Woodstock*, both of which he was writing at the time of trouble. Constable's trustees claimed that, in terms of the agreement already made, the publication of these two works should be theirs, and they worried Sir Walter and wasted his precious hours by taking him to law on the point. He won, but in the winning he showed some *animus*. His counter-claim included a demand for the manuscripts which he had freely given to Constable in 1823. The ground on which he claimed them was that they had been given after a solemn promise that the authorship should not be divulged, and that this promise had not been kept. He even declared that Constable had no right to them.

His worries are pathetic to watch. On 22nd January he definitely gave up hope of retaining Abbotsford, but during January and February he had alternations of hope and despair, that ended in the melancholy satisfaction of remaining. Pitfalls made by cold-blooded wretches lay in his path. Another London publisher, on the verge of bankruptcy, offered a big sum for the publishing rights of *Woodstock*. Happily the solicitor who was now Scott's negotiator got wind of the fact that bankruptcy was impending and refused the offer. *Woodstock* brought Scott's creditors £8500, and it can be imagined what a disheartening it would have been to him if they had been swindled out of it at his very first attempt to repay them.

James Ballantyne went bankrupt, and everything he possessed was sold for the benefit of his creditors, with the exception of his household furniture, which he was allowed to keep. Friends, however, bought the business and installed him as manager ; in half a dozen years James had bought it back for himself out of the profits.

When Cadell, who was an impatient man though outwardly restrained in manner, wanted to distribute the printing of Sir Walter's books among various firms, in order to get them issued quickly, Scott put his foot down and declared that Ballantyne, with whose business he had no longer any connection, should do all his printing. Scott's continuance of trust in James is clear evidence that he held James blameless.

In January and February 1829, James's wife was ill and he himself was so nervous that he could do no work. Sir Walter regarded him and wrote to him with contempt and astonishment that he could not conceal. When Mrs. Ballantyne died on 17th February, James was unable to appear at her funeral, and fled to a quiet corner near Jedburgh, pursued by Sir Walter's reproaches for cowardice. When he came back he took to frequenting the chapel, and it was even reported that he had become a teetotaler, in those days a term of infinite contempt. Accordingly Scott and he drifted away from each other. Joy of life had deserted both of them, and they had no pleasure in each other's discovery of the resource left to the stricken. Ballantyne's vision was sentimental religious contemplation, a farewell to the pleasures that he could no longer enjoy and tearful contemplation of a good time hereafter. Scott's was the proud renunciation of himself, the submission of his mind and body to the deliverance of his honour, stubborn toil in which the very visits of his friends became a menace and inimical. To Ballantyne, meditating only on a reunion with his wife and his favourite child, that seemed as stupid as Ballantyne's evolution was grotesque to Scott.

When Scott's doctors urged him to stop work or to work less, he mocked them. " I am a kettle on the fire and you tell me not to boil." And again, with a touch of satisfaction in his dourness, he parodied :

> " Dour, dour and eident was he ;
>   Dour and eident but and ben ;
>   Dour against their barley-water
>   And eident on the Bramah pen."

Eident is eager and diligent.

They advised him to keep to the annotation of his novels, and had he been capable of restraint the advice might have done him good. But he was hurried along by the tremendous energy of his own organism. Into the last details of his worries, apoplexies, foreign travel, and painful home-coming, I have no desire to go. They do not belong to the pictures of Scott that I should like to paint, and Lockhart has told them with the sombre poignancy that was his highest gift.

INDEX

Abbotsford, 40, 49, 71, 92, 98, 103, 115, 129, 151, 176.
American War of Independence, 17.
— — of 1814, 191.
Anstruther, Philip, 43.
Arrest of Scott for breach of the peace, 67.
Ashestiel, 80, 98, 103, 105, 121.

Baillie, Joanna, 171.
Ballantyne, Alexander, 159.
— James, 70, 101, 144, 155, 161, 166, 192.
— John, 90, 146, 157, 166.
Bath, Sir Walter's stay at, in childhood, 16.
Belches, Williamina, Scott's first love, 27, 30, 31, 73.
Bills, Scott's frequent use of, 15, 199.
Blood-vessel, Scott breaks, at sixteen years old, 19.
Boltfoot, Scott's lame ancestor, 64.
Bonaparte, Scott prophesies that he will bribe the princes and peerage of Britain, 183.
Bower, Johnnie, custodian of Melrose Abbey, 45, 107.
Bowling-green at Abbotsford, 110.
Bruce, John, the piper, 110.
Buccleuch, Duchess of, 55, 180.
— Duke of, 55, 116, 152, 183.
Buchan, Earl of, 140.
Bürger's "Lenore," 29.

Cadell, Robert, Scott's last publisher, 59, 184, 200.
Carlisle, Scott married in St. Mary's, 37.
Carlyle, Thomas, 178.
Castle Street, North, No. 39, 66.
— — South, Scott's first house, 37.
Chantrey's bust of Scott, 62.

Charles I.'s hair, 101, 180.
Charpentier, Charles, Lady Scott's brother, 35, 39.
Children, Scott's, 84.
Clerk of Session, Scott's post as, 182.
Clerk, Will, 20, 46, 68.
Clerks' coach, the, 70.
Clubs frequented by Scott in youth, 20.
Cockburn, Lord, 24.
— Mrs., 5, 167.
Coleridge, 158, 167, 192.
College Wynd, Scott's birthplace, 6.
Constable, the publisher, 39, 57, 122, 146, 152.
Copyrights, Scott's, Constable's losses on, 160, 169.
Covenanters, 80.
Cramp, attacks of, 72, 126.
Cranstoun, Jane Ann, 27.
Criminal trials, Scott's interest in, 24.
Curses, Scott's infrequent, 80.

Dalgleish, butler at Abbotsford, 111.
Debts, Scott's, 41, 160, 199.
De Quincey, 56.
Dogs, Sir Walter's, 69, 113, 129.
Downshire, Lord, guardian of Charlotte Charpentier, 35, 36.
Dryden, Scott's opinion of, 172.

Episcopal Church, Scott's transference to, 189.
Erskine, Will, 27, 50, 165.

Fergusson, Sir Adam, 23, 34, 35, 47, 91, 103, 127.
— Bell, 104.
— Margaret, 104.
Ferrier, James, 43.
First love, 26, 30.
Forbes, Dr. Duncan, 60.
— Sir William, 30.

George IV., coronation of, 190.
George Square, Edinburgh, Scott's home in boyhood and youth, 6.
German prince, episode of, 106.
German, Scott takes classes, 23.
Gilfillan, Rev. George, *Life of Scott*, 35.
Gillies, R. P. 47.

"Hardyknute," ballad of, 167.
High School, Edinburgh, Scott sent to, 17.
Hogg, James, the Ettrick shepherd, 3, 52, 78, 116.
— shepherd at Abbotsford, 55, 108.
Hughes, Mrs., of Uffington, 22, 75.
Hunter, Constable's partner, 58.
Huntly Burn, residence of the Fergussons, 103.
Hurst & Robinson, publishers, 193.

Income, Scott's, as an advocate, 180.
Irving, John, Scott's boyhood companion, 17, 18.
— Washington, 93.
Italian, Scott learns, 18.

Jedburgh, election at, in 1831, 185.
Jeffrey, Lord, 21.
Jobson, Miss, bride of young Walter, 91.
John of Skye, the piper, 56.
— the Lamiter, 64.
Johnson, Samuel, 177, 180.

Laidlaw, William, 52, 107, 120, 183, 185.
Landor, 171.
Lasswade, Scott's first country residence at, 39.
Library at Abbotsford, 59.
Lockhart, John Hugh, Scott's first grandchild, 52.
Lockhart, *Life of Scott*, 2, 3, 20, 69, 87, 118, 169, 175, 182, 192.

Macbeth, butler at Ashestiel, 111.
Mackay, Mrs., housekeeper at Abbotsford, 112.
Mackenzie, author of *The Man of Feeling*, 43, 165.
Macneill, Hector, 168.
Maida, the big hound, 62, 131, 133.
Major Weir (Scott's walking-stick), 119.

Mathieson, Peter, coachman at Abbotsford, 39, 107, 110.
Maturin, Rev. Mr., 169.
Melrose Abbey, 45, 128, 164.
Melville, Lord, 181.
Millar, Miss, governess at Abbotsford, 85.
Miners, habits of, 187.
Mitchell, Rev. Mr., tutor of Scott, 7.
Moore, Thomas, 56, 164.
Morritt of Rokeby, 62, 79, 184.
Murray of Broughton, Prince Charles's secretary, 11.

Painters of Sir Walter, 62.
Parliament House, 23, 24, 115, 182.
Pepys's Diary, 172.
Personality of Sir Walter, 62.
Physical characteristics, 65.
Plummer, Sheriff, 44.
Presbyterian household of the elder Scotts, 8, 189.
Pringle of Torwoodlee, Scott's neighbour, 105.
Purdie, Charlie, 113, 115.
Purdie, Tom, 71, 107, 121, 134.

Radicals, 179, 183, 187.
Raeburn, Sir Henry, 63.
Ramsay, Dean, 189.
Reform Bill, 184.
Riddell, Sir Matthew, washes his head in the christening font, 43.
Rosebank, Uncle Robert Scott's house, 19, 22.
Roslin, Scott's early affection for, 18.
Rutherford, Professor, Scott's maternal grandfather, 7, 16.

Sandyknowe, Scott's earliest consciousness at, 42.
Schiller's *Fiesco*, 24.
Scott, Mrs. Anne, Sir Walter's mother, 4, 14, 18.
Scott, Walter, the elder, 4, 12, 28.
— Robert, uncle of Sir Walter, 19, 39.
— Thomas,   „   „   43.
— Daniel, brother of Sir Walter, 7.
— Major John, „   „   7, 8.
— Robert,   „   „   8, 18, 182.
— Thomas,   „   „   8.

Scott, Anne, sister of Sir Walter, 7.
— Lady, of Abbotsford, 34, 36–7, 84, 114, 118, 172.
— Anne, child of Sir Walter, 95, 132.
— Charles,   ,,   ,,   93, 132.
— Sophia,   ,,   ,,   86.
— Walter,   ,,   ,,   (called Gilnockie), 88, 101, 115, 131
— of Harden, Mrs., 29.
Seward Miss, 64.
Sharpe, Charles Kirkpatrick, 20, 81, 114.
Shelley, 178.
Sheriff of Selkirkshire, Scott's first official position, 39, 80, 181.
Shillinglaw, Joe, carpenter at Darnick, 111, 131.
Shortreed, Robert, 22, 23, 24, 36, 69.
Skene, James, of Rubislaw, 32.
Sleep, Scott's tendency to, 81.
Somerville, Lord, 45.
Speculative Society, 21, 23.
Stewart, Alexander, of Invernahyle, 44.
Stuart, Lady Jane, 27, 32, 73.

Swanston, John, the forester, 74, 111.

Terry, Daniel, 48.
Theatre, Scott's love of, 38, 79.
Thomson, George, tutor at Abbotsford, 85, 115.
Trade Unionists, Scott's persecution of the early, 177, 186.

Volunteer cavalry, Scott organises, 24.

Watson, Tom, 112.
Waverley Novels, 164.
Weavers of Galashiels, 188.
Wellington, Duke of, 179.
Wilkie, the painter, 141.
Wine-drinking, Scott's habit of, in youth, 20.
Winnos, John, sub-oracle of Abbotsford, 111, 139.
Wordsworth, 56, 71, 92, 101, 170, 175.

Yair, Thomas the butler at, 117.

PRINTED IN GREAT BRITAIN BY
MORRISON & GIBB LTD., EDINBURGH